GW00888986

Terrariums

Terrariums

An easy guide to growing a host of miniature gardens using traditional terrariums, glass bottles and decorative dishes.

PAMELA WESTLAND

THE
APPLE
PRESS

A QUINTET BOOK

Published by The Apple Press
6 Blundell Street
London N7 9BH

ISBN 1-85076-452-2

This book was designed and produced by
Quintet Publishing Limited
6 Blundell Street
London N7 9BH

Project Editor: Laura Sandelson
Creative Director: Richard Dewing
Designer: Ian Hunt
Editor: Lydia Darbyshire
Illustrator: Ivan Hissey
Photographer: Nelson Hargreaves

Typeset in Great Britain by
Central Southern Typesetters, Eastbourne
Manufactured in Singapore by Eray Scan Pte. Ltd.
Printed in Hong Kong by Leefung-Asco Printers Ltd.

ACKNOWLEDGEMENTS

We are grateful to Glass-Style Creations, Unit D3,
Taylor Industrial Estate, Warrington Road, Risley,
Warrington WA3 6BL, UK, for the loan of the leaded-
glass terrariums that are featured in some of
the projects.
We are grateful to W. Hobby Ltd, Knights Hill Square,
London SE27 0HH for supplying the terrarium kit
featured on page 13.

Contents

Introduction

Growing plants in a terrarium or a dish garden makes possible the cultivation of a wide range of plant types. The enclosed, controlled environment of a terrarium, a bottle garden or a bell-jar is ideally suited to all those plants – ferns, mosses, bromeliads and others – that thrive in a level of humidity that can rarely be achieved in normal domestic living conditions. A dish garden, on the other hand, which has been provided with adequate drainage and placed in a sunny or bright position, will enable you to grow plants such as forest and desert cacti, alpines and herbs that prefer warm, dry conditions.

The art – or more accurately the science – of terrarium gardening was discovered by accident in the mid-19th century by an amateur botanist, Dr Nathaniel Bagshaw Ward, who had tried and failed to raise rare ferns in the heavily polluted atmosphere of his garden in London's docklands. It was not until Dr Ward used a closed bottle for a different purpose – he wanted to observe the development of moths – that, without even trying, he at last succeeded in raising a species of fern that had until then resisted his endeavours. Not only that, he made the important observation that the moisture in the bottle was regularly and naturally recycled. The moisture vapour given off by the damp soil during the warmest part of the day condensed on the inside of the glass and gradually trickled down the glass and back into the soil.

It is this re-enactment of the rain cycle in closed containers that makes them suitable for plants that might otherwise have difficulty in adapting successfully to the artificial living conditions imposed on them in open indoor gardens. Moisture is given off by the plants' leaves, it evaporates in the trapped air, clings to the glass in the form of condensation and is reabsorbed by the soil, where it is ready to be taken up again by the plants' roots. The diagram on page 35 shows this cycle clearly.

Dr Ward's further experiments, which included growing a fern in a bottle for nearly four years without any additional water or any

LEFT Wardian cases are miniature greenhouses. They are named after Dr Nathaniel Ward who discovered, by chance, that ferns need a humid atmosphere and protection from smoke and draughts in order to grow successfully. Ward proceeded to build many different fern cases of varying shapes.

attention whatsoever, eventually gave rise to the use of enclosed plant cases, called Wardian cases, for the transportation of plants. The use of these glass cases, many of them as elaborate as the glasshouses in botanical gardens, enabled botanists and explorers to bring home new plants from all over the world without the usual ratio of loss or damage. The glass structures protected the plants not only from careless handling but also from the effects of temperature changes, salt spray and drying winds. Furthermore, to the delight of their sponsors, the plants actually thrived and developed during the long voyages and arrived in peak condition.

To emphasize the importance of his scientific discovery, at the Great Exhibition in London's Crystal Palace in 1851 Dr Ward exhibited a bottle planted with healthy ferns and mosses that, he said, had at that time not been watered for 18 years. The decorative properties of a collection of healthy plants growing in glass cases or bottles started a new craze in interior design, and indoor gardening, and Wardian cases became the focal point in many fashionable Victorian drawing-rooms.

Like ferns languishing in partial shade, however, the fashion for bottle gardening eventually went into partial decline, but it has recently enjoyed an enthusiastic revival. Several

companies now make elegant, Victorian-inspired terrariums, some of which closely resemble the early Wardian cases, and some produce kits for people who want to make their own. Alternatively, you can begin your indoor gardening as Dr Ward did in an enclosed bottle, a carboy or a wide variety of other containers, some of which are familiar household items.

The different needs of plants grown in enclosed containers and in dish gardens, the drainage and growing media, the temperature, light, humidity and moisture requirements, and the range of plant types that are suitable are discussed fully in the following chapters. It would be unwise to expect to emulate Dr Ward's success without making an effort to balance the moisture and maintain the plants in good order. The Directory of plants at the back of this book may help you to plan a group of plants that, in either a terrarium or a dish garden, should be able to coexist healthily.

Indoor gardening is a hobby you can enjoy at any level, from raising a single plant in a preserve jar to planting an impressive collection in a miniature conservatory, from growing two or three sturdy cacti in a saucer to creating a stylish or stylized dish garden that is a study in texture and colour contrast. It is a hobby you can enjoy at any time of the year and one that can enhance any room in the home.

CHAPTER ONE

Terrariums and Other Glass Containers

When you think of glass in terms of a container for growing plants you may think first, or even solely, of a purpose-made terrarium of the leaded panel type or of a large carboy or bottle garden. However, that would be to restrict the opportunities that growing plants in or under glass can offer and to deny yourself part of the creative enjoyment of the hobby. Once you start thinking laterally, you will probably find that you have already got several containers in your home, and car boot sales, junk shops and street markets will prove to be happy hunting grounds where, for a relatively small outlay, you will be able to increase your repertoire still further. Anything from a large brandy glass displaying a single pink and white flowering African violet (*Saintpaulia*) to a discarded glass salad or fruit bowl sheltering a medley of foliage plants can become an open and improvised terrarium in the broadest sense of the word.

TERRARIUMS

Reverting to the strictest sense of the word – a glass container that completely encloses a growing plant or collection of plants in a sealed environment – a terrarium can vary from an elaborate representation of a tropical plant house in a botanical garden to a simple cube with a pointed roof. Between these extremes lie almost every conceivable size and shape, including some free-standing models and others designed to be wall mounted.

These glasshouses are made of variously shaped, sometimes coloured, pieces of glass held together with strips of copper foil. This type of terrarium has "antique" connotations largely because the construction style is strongly reminiscent of the leaded-light windows found in some old cottages and houses. The good news is that they look just as much at home in a modern setting as in a

RIGHT With the slanting roof in place, the terrarium is complete. The sunbeams highlight the sheen of the healthy plants and emphasize the different leaf textures and colours.

BELOW RIGHT A terrarium fitted with a detachable roof makes planting and maintenance much easier. This terrarium made of wood is one of the less traditional styles available.

LEFT A small leaded terrarium with a pointed roof, a green glass bottle, glass-stoppered preserving jars and a wine carafe demonstrate the wide variety of containers that can be used as terrariums.

traditional one. Stand a richly planted glasshouse on a starkly modern table in front of a large picture window – an ideal situation for it – and it will naturally become a focal point of the room.

You can buy different styles of leaded terrariums in garden centres and specialist garden shops, where they are likely to be sold ready planted, and in some department stores and interior design shops. Look for them, too, in second-hand shops. You may be lucky enough to find one at a fraction of the original cost.

Another option, which is also a reasonably inexpensive way of acquiring a traditional terrarium, is to make one from a kit. This course has the added potential of increasing the satisfaction and pride you feel in your new acquisition. You do not need any special skill to construct a neat and tidy container except the twin assets of confidence and patience, and you have to add only one specialist tool to the kit package, a heavy-duty, 75-Watt soldering iron.

Terrarium kits may be bought at hobby shops, some specialist garden shops and by mail order. A typical kit will consist of pre-cut glass shapes, some of which may be coloured to form a decorative border, a roll each of copper foil and soldering tin, a set of lead profiles where appropriate, a pattern and a sheet of detailed building instructions. A kit for a hanging model would also include a set of chains and hooks.

Makers of terrarium kits stress that an extra pair of hands to help keep the construction rigid at a part-way stage is more important than any amount of craft ability, and so it is perhaps best to consider such a venture as a potential team effort or family enterprise. It must be stressed, however, that children should never be put in charge of, or left holding, a hot soldering iron.

The first stage of the task, which is illustrated in detail on page 13, is to edge each piece of

ABOVE This elegant terrarium is large enough to contain many plants.

filling in and disguising gaps and deficiencies. A few little lumps and bumps will only serve to emphasize that the glasshouse is an example of hand-craftsmanship.

If the experience you gain in building a terrarium kit gives your confidence and enthusiasm a strong enough boost, you might care to advance to the next stage and construct a glasshouse from a pattern. Some hobby specialists sell these, the craft equivalent of a dress pattern, for a range of terrarium designs from a small hanging basket to a symmetrical dolls' house style. Each pattern folder contains detailed instructions and full-size shapes from which you can cut out the glass pieces yourself. This allows you to select the colour and quality of the glass you want – colours range from carmine red and violet to light blue and ultramarine – but it does mean that you will need more tools. A good-quality glass cutter and glass breaking tongs are considered essential, and you must wear goggles to protect your eyes from any splinters that might fly off while you are cutting the glass.

BOTTLE GARDENS

The second main type of enclosed container is a carboy or one of its derivatives, popularly known as a bottle garden. The large, balloon-shaped jars of thick, clear glass, which were originally made to transport acid and other corrosive liquids, were found to be the perfect shape for planting. The top opening is wide enough to allow you to use your hand for planting – a much easier and more hands-on method than using slender tools – and the jars are wide enough to allow attractively wide and side-trailing plants to be included.

The original acid jars have been superseded in commercial use by other, more secure

glass with copper foil, a sticky, even tacky material. You place an edge of a piece of pre-cut glass in the centre of the strip, press it down firmly and fold up both edges so that they cling evenly and smoothly to the glass. When all the glass pieces have been outlined with copper foil the task of assembly begins. It is important at this stage to follow the pattern closely, since pieces of pre-cut glass, like those of a jigsaw puzzle, can look remarkably alike.

Each piece of glass is soldered along the edge and, two by two, the adjoining sections are pressed firmly together. For a beginner perhaps the most taxing part of the construction is to achieve a thin, neat line of solder, but this does come with practice. In any case, the first stages, the construction of the base of the design, will be obscured by gravel, compost and plants, and solder has the accommodating property of

Making a Terrarium from a Kit

You can increase your pleasure in your terrarium by making it yourself from a kit. A variety of styles is available from specialist hobby shops and by mail order.

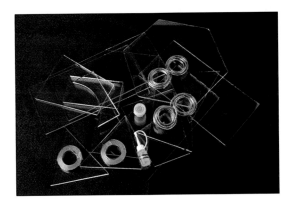

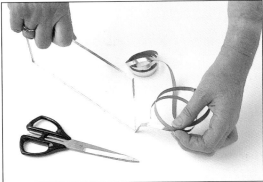

1 The kit we used consisted of pre-cut glass shapes, two rolls of copper foil, two rolls of soldering tin, a tin of soldering paste, a bottle of patina and an instruction sheet.

2 Press the copper foil on to the edge of the glass. Begin at the centre of one edge so that the joins are less obvious.

3 Fold over the copper foil to both sides of the glass. Run along the surface of the foil with a pencil to ensure that there are no air bubbles.

4 To construct this design, five glass strips are placed side by side along the battens and held in place with two strips of adhesive tape.

YOU WILL NEED

- terrarium kit
- scissors
- pencil
- adhesive tape
- ruler
- 2 pieces of batten held together in

- an L-shape
- 75-Watt soldering iron
- 4 drawing pins (thumb tacks)
- card
- soft cloth

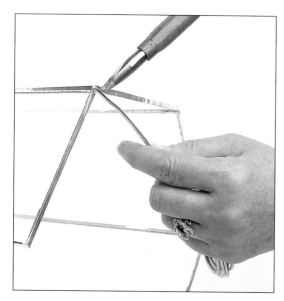

7 The completed terrarium is planted with a Cretan brake fern (Pteris *cretica*), a weeping fig (*Ficus benjamina*), a polka-dot plant (*Hypoestes* *sanguinolenta*) and a maidenhair fern (*Adiantum raddianum*).

5 The five pieces of glass forming the sides are placed on top of the base and temporarily held in place with adhesive tape, then the sill and the front arch are put in position. Solder is applied at each corner.

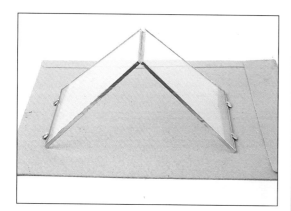

6 The roof is constructed on a piece of card and held in position with drawing pins (thumb tacks). At this stage apply the patina to the lead with a soft cloth if you want a burnished-copper finish. We left ours without patina.

containers, and so they are frequently on sale in garden centres, markets and even antique shops. They are, however, probably too large and cumbersome for small homes, and, when they are fully planted they can be heavy and awkward to move.

Similarly shaped but smaller containers are now manufactured specially for planting. Some of these are made of clear glass, which admits the maximum amount of light and permits the greatest degree of visibility. Other styles, in various shades of green and largely manufactured in Spain and Italy, give the plant collection the exotic appearance of the jungle. Such jars, however, admit a restricted amount of light and need to be positioned near a particularly good light source for at least part of every day or every week.

Glass bottles may be fitted with a matching glass stopper – many of them are sold in that way – or with a thick cork disc. Alternatively, they may be used with the top open, an

LEFT Jars of almost all shapes and sizes can be transformed into terrariums. Here you see a storage jar, a confectionery jar, a cider jug and a wine glass filled with living plants.

BELL-JARS AND HAND-LIGHTS

The method of creating a controlled and agreeable environment for growing plants in containers indoors was adapted in the 18th century for those grown out of doors. Paradoxically, two items specifically manufactured then for exterior use have become collectors' items today and are now being used for indoor plants.

The first of these was the bell-jar, a large, heavy and unwieldy dome made of thick glass. Some models had ventilation holes and covers in the top so that the temperature and humidity could be regulated; others had a knob or handle for lifting.

The other predecessor of the cloche, known as the hand-light, had much in common with a leaded terrarium and, like the terrarium, was made in a wide range of designs. Hand-lights were constructed of small panes of glass fixed with putty or metal strips to iron, zinc or copper frames or, for ease of dismantling, simply bolted together. Both the design and the complexity of the construction varied, and you may find examples in antique shops or interior design shops that are cone, pyramid or bell shaped, or that resemble a storm lantern, a miniature house or a modern cloche.

If you are able to buy a bell-jar or a hand-light, you can use it as a removable cover not for tiny seedlings and tender outdoor plants as was originally intended, but for a glorious indoor plant display. Choose a shallow dish that is slightly larger than the cover for the planter, compose the display and put the cover in place. If you have achieved the correct balance of growing medium, plants and water you should need to lift the lid only to remove damaged or fading leaves or, eventually, to freshen the display with one or two replacement plants.

ABOVE A tall, round storage jar, complete with cork stopper, provides agreeable humidity for the frilly leaved parsley ivy, the spectacular pink-and-green-leaved polka-dot plant (Hypoestes sanguinolenta), a low-growing selaginella and a miniature hebe.

attractive option if you wish to grow one or two especially slender plants. This open-top approach to container growing, while obviously not creating a sealed environment, does not significantly affect the humidity enjoyed by the plants, and very little additional watering should be necessary. This is because the shape of the jar – the wide girth and narrow neck – encourages condensation to form on the inside of the glass, trickle down and keep the compost permanently moist.

BELL-JARS AND HAND-LIGHTS

Items used outdoors by gardeners in the 18th and 19th centuries are now highly prized containers for indoor gardens. Some bell-jars have removable covers at the top so that the temperature and humidity may be controlled. Hand-lights vary widely in their style of construction, but many have the leaded-pane appearance of a modern terrarium. Heavy glass, pear-shaped containers usually have an aperture that prevents them being used for wholly closed arrangements, but they do, nevertheless, provide higher levels of humidity and more constant temperatures than are possible with open displays.

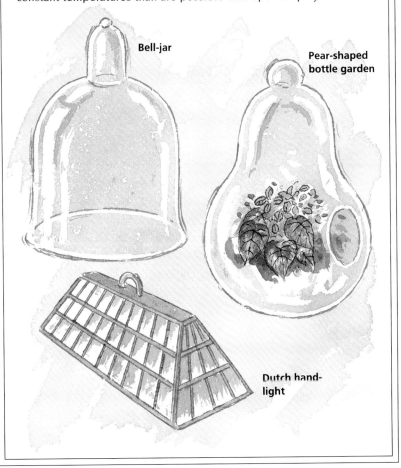

Bell-jar

Pear-shaped bottle garden

Dutch hand-light

Other glass covers made for other purposes may be adapted in a similar way to enclose a single indoor plant or a collection. Look in antique shops and second-hand shops for Victorian glass domes, which were made to protect dried flower arrangements from dust, skeleton-clock covers and cheese dishes with flat-topped glass covers (protect the wood with a pottery planter) or the type of inexpensive plastic dome sold to cover food. This latter type can be useful for experimental indoor gardens, but knowledgeable growers will soon find fault with it, since moisture tends to cling to plastic rather than trickle down the sides. Furthermore, the slightest scratch on a plastic cover, made perhaps with a planting tool, is exaggerated and made more noticeable by the way it catches the light.

AQUARIUMS

If you have set your sights on a container that will allow the plants room to grow, an aquarium may be just what you need. New ones are relatively expensive, but advertisements in local newspapers, for sale notices in local shops and even car boot sales and jumble sales can alert you to the opportunities offered by used bargains.

If you find an aquarium complete with a glass top, so much the better. If not, you can have a sheet of glass cut to fit. Most aquariums have a ledge just inside the rim to support a cover, and it is simply a case of measuring and cutting to achieve a close fit. The better the fit the more difficult it will be to remove the glass. Never try to prise it up with a knife blade or a spoon handle. One neat and unobtrusive way of solving this problem is to stick a large, clear glass marble to the glass at each end to make sturdy, almost invisible handles.

RIGHT This antique wrought-iron Wardian case protects delicate ferns from draughts and dry air and maintains the steady, humid environment that they prefer.

than to put in the drainage and soil layers, carefully and artistically arrange the plants and give them their once-and-for-all-time watering – and then to discover a persistent leak.

An aquarium with an interior light, which many of them have, not only enhances a plant display but also improves the health and rate of growth of the plants. If you buy a second-hand aquarium with a fluorescent light fitting check the wiring carefully or ask a knowledgeable person to do so. You can buy light fittings specifically made for aquarium use from pet and aquarium shops and from some garden centres. Do not buy an ordinary fluorescent tube of the kind sold for domestic use. These are not suitable for aquariums.

Other, smaller containers that were designed to create a less than tropical environment for fish can also be used for plants. Rectangular fish tanks small enough to make a focal point on a windowsill or a talking point as a table centrepiece can be used open or covered with a piece of glass. Artistically planted with a contrasting selection of ground-cover plants and taller specimens, they can offer all the variety and much of the appeal of their larger counterparts.

Fat, chubby goldfish bowls are ideally suited to imaginative plantings of, for example, a variety of selaginella, a small-leaved ivy and a maidenhair fern. In a small bowl it may be better to restrict the planting to a single specimen, choosing perhaps an African violet, a golden-leaved *Soleirolia soleirolii* or a miniature form of *Fittonia verschaffeltii* var. *argyroneura*. Goldfish bowls, too, may be used open, or they could be closed with a well-fitting piece of bevelled glass. It will depend on the type of plants you wish to grow, and whether you enjoy the spectacle of the more vigorous specimens reaching ever upwards.

The shape and proportions of an aquarium – a rectangle with a large, flat top – have a significant effect on the way moisture collects and is redistributed. Condensation tends to collect under the lid and to drip down vertically, rather than to run down the container sides as it does with domed or pitched roof styles. If this becomes a problem you may have to lift off the top each day and wipe it dry, replacing the lost moisture by judicious watering from time to time.

An aquarium may have been discarded because it was no longer watertight – a property that is important whether it is to house fish or plants. Any deficiencies in this respect can be quickly and effectively made good by using an aquarium sealant. It may seem obvious, but do check that the container is watertight before you plant it. There is nothing more irritating

LEFT The round, robust shape of a glass goldfish bowl is well suited to low-growing plants with a side-trailing habit. For their contrasting leaf colours and textures we chose a maidenhair fern (*Adiantum raddianum*), a polka-dot plant (*Hypoestes sanguinolenta*) and a creeping fig (*Ficus pumila*).

Glass food and drink containers offer good opportunities for spur-of-the-moment planting experiments, since most of us have at least one or two suitable items in our homes. Once you have recognized their potential as bottle gardens in disguise it is simply a matter of matching them up with appropriate plants.

Glass food jars make a good starting point, especially for children, and even a humble honey or pickle jar can become a decorative and effective planter. Small jars are best used for a single specimen plant. Mosses and ferns are particularly suitable subjects, and if the jars are kept in a reasonably accessible place, such as on a kitchen table or a windowsill, they will form a constantly changing display. The growth and development of mosses are fascinating to watch, while the development of a fern through the various stages of its life cycle – from spore to prothallus, gametophyte and sporophyte – is

BELOW A glass teapot, more usually employed in the making of herbal teas, makes a striking container for a trio of low-growing plants. Our choice was a polka-dot plant (*Hypoestes sanguinolenta*), a selaginella and a dwarf creeping fig (*Ficus pumila* "Minima").

"SHIP IN A BOTTLE"

To plant a jar on its side, when the headroom is limited, you will have to select dwarf forms of plants such as *Fittonia verschaffeltii* var. *argyroneura*, selaginellas and attractive mosses. Their large openings make these jars simple to plant because even an adult can easily reach into them with a hand and arm.

The same cannot be said of wine bottles, whose narrow necks make the insertion of even the smallest-leaved plants something of a challenge. If you do want to create the horticultural equivalent of a ship in a bottle and if you are adept at using chopsticks, look for a plant with the properties of a dwarf creeping fig (*Ficus pumila*). If the planted and stoppered bottle is placed on its side the plant will gradually reach from end to end and create an attractive long, low display. You can give it the benefit of strong light by housing it on a windowsill, but when visitors arrive move it to a coffee table or the dining table where it can provoke delight, astonishment and disbelief.

A wine bottle, turned on its side and planted with a low-growing species, will make an attractive and effective closed container.

a biology lesson in itself. To create ideal growing conditions for mosses and ferns, use screw-topped jars or, to admit more light, cover the tops with transparent plastic film or jam-jar covers.

Larger food jars offer more scope for proportionately larger plants, and the biggest ones have two potential uses. You can use them upright, planted with one or two tall slender plants, or place them on their sides to display a selection of compact, low-growing specimens.

The largest glass jars of all, of the kind that were used in sweet shops, have now been replaced by plastic ones. These can be used for

gleaming clarity with rice and water. Put in about 50g/2 tablespoons of dry, uncooked rice, half fill the decanter with cold water and cover the opening with one hand. Shake the decanter vigorously until the opaque film has been removed. Then you can fully appreciate the subtle blues, greens, yellows and reds of the foliage plants you select.

Most drinking glasses are too small to encourage enthusiastic planting, but large brandy balloons, sometimes called brandy snifters, have decorative planting potential. Because they are raised on a short stem, which makes a miniature pedestal, they are especially suitable for highlighting a single flowering plant such as an African violet or a kalanchoe. The wide open neck of the glass gives ready access to the plant and makes it easy to remove flowers as they fade or die. If you prefer a mixed arrangement you could choose three plants from a range of dwarf succulents.

The broad opening of such containers has a disadvantage, too, since it allows a considerable degree of evaporation and, consequently, rapid drying out of the compost. It is in just these circumstances that some people fall into the trap of over-watering. The compost must be allowed to dry out, but only just, before further, small quantities of water are added.

For this type of open display, when the container is less a terrarium, more a glass plant pot, a number of suitable items comes to mind. You could use a glass comport, which is, in effect, a fruit bowl raised on a stand; a shallow bowl, which could be covered with a glass lid; or a wide, deep glass vase. Tulip-shaped glass candle stands, known as storm lanterns, glass teapots, mixing bowls and toughened glass saucepans could all be used as decorative planters.

planting and, since they may be yours for the asking in your local store, they too make good first-time planters. Plastic jars do, however, have similar drawbacks to plastic domes – both scratching and inner moisture spread are problems.

If you decide to use food jars upright, you could plant them with a selection of herbs, which is an ideal project for a kitchen windowsill and a means of producing fresh aromatic leaves throughout the year. Chives are an especially successful and attractive subject to grow in this way.

Decanters can make stylish and individual bottle gardens. The broad-based ship's decanter shape offers the widest scope for planting, but it is important to avoid the situation that can arise when a number of plants that fit comfortably around the base grow tall enough to crowd the neck opening. If you buy a second-hand container that has become stained in use it can be brought back to

CHAPTER TWO

Planting a Terrarium

Planting a terrarium or a glass container of any kind has much in common with composing a flower arrangement. If the display is to be pleasing and look balanced the plants must be in proportion to the container and to each other, they must have an adequate and consistent source of moisture and they must be in prime condition. In a terrarium, as in a flower arrangement, one damaged or diseased leaf or dead flower can spoil an otherwise flawless group.

Growing plants in a restricted or enclosed environment puts particular emphasis on every aspect of planting: on the drainage material, the growing medium, the moisture balance, the planting method – the right tools for the job make all the difference, especially when access to the container is limited – and lastly the suitability and health of the plants themselves. The Directory at the end of the book should help you to make a choice of decorative plants appropriate to the container of your choice. The other aspects are dealt with here.

DRAINAGE AND COMPOST

Unlike flower pots, glass containers have no drainage holes and therefore no built-in means of getting rid of excess moisture. It is essential, therefore, to provide a drainage medium, and a double layer is recommended for the purpose. First of all you need sufficient washed or pea gravel or, if that is not obtainable, coarse grit, to cover the base of the terrarium to a depth of 2.5cm/1in. Then you need a similar depth of charcoal. You can use horticultural charcoal, which is usually obtainable from garden centres, or the type used for aquarium filters. You can even use ordinary barbecue charcoal, but you will need to break it up into smaller pieces. This twin layer is absolutely essential for

CROSS SECTION OF A BOTTLE GARDEN

It is essential that a closed container such as a carboy has a double layer of drainage material under the compost. Use a paper funnel or cone to introduce the gravel, charcoal and compost to the carboy so that the glass does not get smeared and dirty.

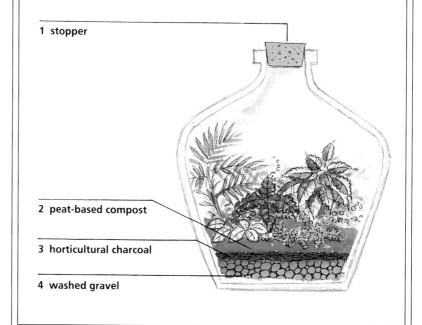

1 stopper

2 peat-based compost

3 horticultural charcoal

4 washed gravel

healthy plant growth. Not only does it provide drainage, but it also absorbs gases and helps to prevent the growing medium from becoming stagnant.

The type of compost you choose will depend on the type and style of the container and the plants you intend growing. Essentially the choice is between a peat-based compost and a loam-based one or, in some cases, a mixture of the two. Whatever you choose, the growing medium must be completely free of weed seeds

RIGHT A trio of African violets *(Saintpaulia)* makes a colourful group, especially when displayed in a glistening glass container. This green, footed dish is a comport dating from the 1940s.

and diseases – soil scooped up from the garden will not do!

Peat-based composts, which are light and clean to handle, contain few nutrients and these will need to be supplemented by the use of a slow-release fertilizer. Both the type that is mixed with the compost before planting and pellets that are pushed into the compost close to the plants are preferable to fertilizer granules, which are sprinkled on the surface. These look like an obvious afterthought to the display and can seem obtrusive. Liquid feeding is not an option in an enclosed container because the compost would rapidly become waterlogged and have no way of drying out. It may not, however, be necessary to fertilize healthy plants very often. Feeding promotes growth and hastens the time when your carefully selected plant collection has to be pruned or replaced because it has outgrown its environment. Some commercial growers now even use dwarfing chemicals to retard the growth of terrarium plants.

Loam-based composts make it easier to achieve and maintain the correct moisture balance, and for this reason they are preferable, especially in wide-necked containers such as open fish tanks or salad bowls. Most bromeliads and succulents tend to do better in this medium or in a mixture of peat and loam. Ferns, on the other hand, tend to do better in a peat-based compost, as long as it is never allowed to dry out completely.

Whichever type of compost you use, you will need to insert a layer about 7.5cm/3in deep in a medium-sized terrarium or bottle garden and proportionately less in smaller containers.

TOOLS AND EQUIPMENT

Before you begin planting it is important to have all the necessary equipment to hand so that you can concentrate on the design and style of your indoor garden without having to break off to look for a makeshift spear, dibber or fork.

BELOW Some of the extended tools that can be used for planting bottle gardens and other narrow-necked containers: a spoon becomes a trowel, a fork is used as a rake and together they make tongs. A cotton reel can be used as a tamping stick, a razor blade as a knife and a darning needle or other narrow implement as a spear for fallen leaves. The sponge is invaluable for cleaning or removing excess moisture from the inside of the glass.

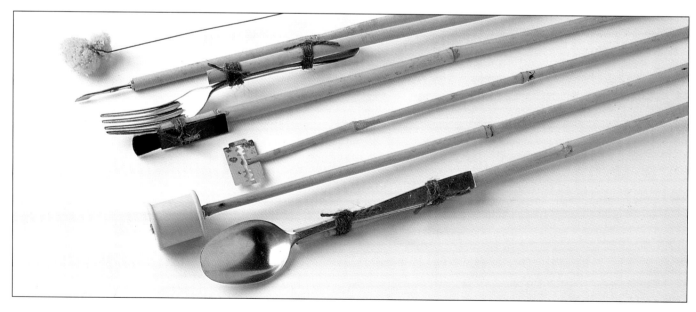

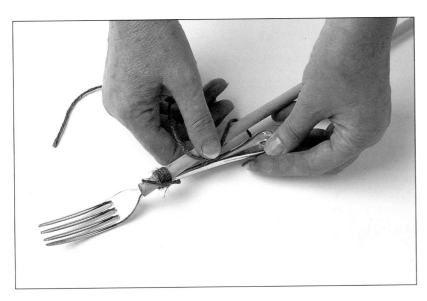

ABOVE A fork lashed with twine to a length of cane can be used as a miniature rake or, with an extended spoon, as one element in a pair of tongs when planting a narrow-necked container.

If you are planting a container with a wide opening which allows you to use your hands, this will minimize the items you require. Not only that, you may find it more therapeutic to use your hands to scoop holes in the compost and to firm in the plants – hands-on experience in a literal sense.

As a rule, the larger the aperture of the container the fewer specialist or improvised tools you will need; the narrower the opening of the bottle garden the more ingenious – and deft – you will need to be.

It is possible to buy miniature tools for indoor gardening, but many of these have standard-length handles, which are not long enough to reach the base of a terrarium, bottle or jar. Improvisation is usually the order of the day therefore, and can, in its way, add to the satisfaction of the planting. You will be able to make most of the tools you need from everyday household items bound firmly to a length of garden cane. The smaller the aperture, the smaller the tool will need to be; the deeper the container, the longer the cane.

Spoons of various shapes and sizes make efficient scoops, which you can use to make indentations in the compost. Choose one that is appropriate to the size of the aperture – a grapefruit spoon or a teaspoon would be suitable for a wine decanter, while a dessertspoon or tablespoon would be better for a carboy. Spoons with straight rather than curved handles are best, since they will lie flat against the cane and be easiest to manoeuvre.

Cut a piece of garden cane that will be long enough to reach the base of the container when the full length of the spoon handle, not just the tip, is strapped to it. Bind the handle to the cane in two places, once at the tip and once close to the bowl. You can use fine string, twine or garden twine. If the spoon is expendable and it does not matter if it gets scratched, fine wire, such as fuse wire or florist's silver wire, can be used.

An old table fork lashed to a length of cane in a similar way has a variety of uses. It can be used with a spoon as the other half of a pair of tongs to grip plants as they are lowered into a container. When the aperture is too narrow to permit the use of the two implements, a fork can be used alone, the prongs spearing the soil surrounding the roots and taking a firm grip on the plant. An extended fork can also be used to scratch and aerate the surface of the compost – an essential part of bottle garden maintenance – and to spear fallen leaves or other unwanted matter that may spoil the appearance of the display.

A smaller, more precise tool for picking up fallen leaves is a darning needle inserted into a length of cane or, like the spoon and fork, firmly lashed to it. A needle used in this way becomes a precision tool that will enable you to pick up the smallest items, even an unsightly lump in the compost, and also to adjust the position of

A razor blade inserted securely into a slit in the base of a cane becomes an effective craft knife or scalpel, which can be used to prune over-sized plants or to remove dead leaves or stems. Once the unwanted material is severed from the plant, a needle or fork can be used to remove it.

If the container opening is not wide enough to allow you to use your fingers to firm in the plants – an important part of the planting process if they are to get a firm hold on life – you can make a serviceable substitute with an empty cotton reel. Pare the end of a piece of cane so that it fits tightly in the hole and push the reel firmly on to it. The importance of firmly securing the improvised tools to their makeshift handles cannot be over emphasized. It is anything but therapeutic to have to use one tool after another in an attempt to retrieve one that has slipped its fastenings. At that point, ingenuity and improvisation become less a challenge, more an irritating diversion.

The last piece of do-it-yourself equipment you are likely to need for the maintenance of a terrarium is a means of cleaning the inside of the glass. This is a task you should not neglect. The slightest film or streak of soil can detract considerably from the attractiveness of the plant display, and, at worst, it can cut down on the light penetration. A small piece of natural sponge or plastic foam bound to the end of stout but pliable wire makes an ideal glass cleaner. Twist the wire securely round and round the centre of the sponge, pinching it into an hour-glass shape and, again, making sure that it cannot break free.

ABOVE A large jar is transformed into a piece of living sculpture. A delicate touch, patience and small, long-handled tools are necessary to pot the plants through such a narrow opening.

a leaf, flower or stem. You may find, for example, that by moving a bottle garden from place to place you disturb the angle of a plant, or that a plant grows unevenly and obscures part of another one. Careful wielding of a needle may be all that is required to restore the display to order.

SELECTING THE PLANTS

If your display is to consist of three or more plants, it is a good idea to have a planting plan so that you can be sure that the arrangement will be as pleasing and natural looking as possible. A simple if unmathematical way of doing this is to cut out a piece of paper the size of the planting area – that is, the base of the terrarium or bottle garden – and to take it with you when you go to buy the plants. You can stand a selection of plants on the paper, move them around and swap them over until you achieve a grouping you like.

If you are buying small or medium-sized plants, bear in mind that, even with the minimum of nutrients in the compost, they will eventually increase in size. If the terrarium has a maximum girth much greater than that of the base – as a carboy does – it may be helpful to have this measurement, too, so that you can readily assess the growth area available. Do not select any plants that even at this stage exceed the maximum girth, which means that they

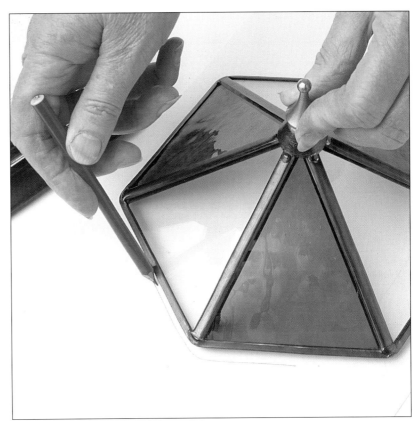

RIGHT In close-up, one can appreciate the varied planting and the graduation of heights that make the most of a container of this quality.

ABOVE Draw round the outline of the container, in this case a hexagonal terrarium, and cut a paper pattern to the shape. This will help you to buy the plants of the appropriate size.

LANDSCAPING

If the container is going to be viewed from only one angle, you may want to landscape the planting arrangement by having a greater depth of compost in one corner or towards the back and using the principle of low plants being set at the front. Remember that carefully placed rocks, stones and shells can immeasurably enhance the appearance of the plants.

consider that air plants – tillandsias – would create a suitable effect, especially if they were planted in an angular container such as a leaded terrarium. A group of three such plants, with their clearly defined outlines, would make a striking and unusual display.

You might consider that a hothouse look is best characterized by red-leaved plants and those whose foliage is heavily veined or tinged with red. In this case you might choose plants such as painted net leaf (*Fittonia verschaffeltii*), with its dramatic red, green and white foliage, *Pilea spruceana*, with its red and grey-green stripes, *Cryptanthus acaulis*, which is like a red and green star cluster, and *Peperomia Clusiifolia* "Jeli", a plant with heavily variegated yellow and green leaves outlined in red.

Ferns of all kinds may suggest the moist, intriguing and varied undergrowth of a forest floor and offer plenty of colour and leaf-shape variety for a bottle garden. You might include tall ferns such as *Nephrolepis exaltata*, the cloudy, misted outline of an adiantum, a button fern (*Pellaea rotundifolia*) if space allows it to spread, and the substantial silhouette and robust form of a bird's nest fern (*Asplenium nidus*).

The compact forms of selaginellas may be grouped together to suggest an undersea environment, which can be especially suitable in a shallow, sealed container when the hummocky plants seem to resemble clumps of seaweed. In a shallow fish tank or a large glass bottle displayed on its side you could include a prostrate variety, *Selaginella kraussiana* "Aurea", *S. martensii*, which, with its open-hand-like foliage, bears a remarkable resemblance to some types of seaweed and *S. apoda*, which forms neat mounds. Two or three interesting pieces of rock or large, tide-smoothed stones positioned among the plants would further the marine-like illusion.

would touch the glass and might become diseased or be bent or broken by contact with it.

Certain plants may suggest a theme for your indoor gardens, although such notions, like beauty, tend to be in the eye of the beholder and specific associations vary from one gardener to another.

If you wished to create a fantasy garden of exotic and mysterious shapes you might

LEFT If the equivalent of a ship-in-a-bottle appeals to you, guide the gravel, charcoal and compost through the aperture by means of a paper cone. Choose slender plants with flexible stems and soft leaves to facilitate the planting.

HOW TO PLANT A TERRARIUM

If you are planting a terrarium such as an aquarium, a wide-necked bowl or any other glass container to which you have easy access, you will not need any special means of guiding in or levelling the gravel, charcoal and compost. When you are planting a narrow-necked container such as a small carboy or decanter, however, a funnel or paper cone will be needed to allow you to build up the layers evenly without the materials touching and soiling the inside of the glass. You will find that it is difficult to remove streaks of compost that appear on the sides without using a trickle of water, which may upset the moisture balance.

Have ready everything you will need for planting, and arrange the plants, still in their pots, on the paper plan of the container for the last time. Move them around until you are happy with the balance of height, leaf colour and texture. Remember to take into account the angle from which the terrarium will be viewed. If it will always be standing against a wall or screen, the tallest plants should be at the back, with the others in graduating heights down to the shortest in the front. If the terrarium is likely to be viewed from all sides, as it may be on a coffee table, position the tallest plant in the centre, with the others graded in height all around.

Using a paper cone or funnel if necessary, gradually pour in the gravel or grit to form the first layer. Shake the container gently to spread it evenly. Add the charcoal in a similar way. If you are planting a bottle garden or a narrow-necked container, you can spread the charcoal by raking it with a fork on a cane. Finally, add the compost and spread it evenly to a depth of 5–7.5cm/2–3in. If the terrarium is to be viewed from only one angle, you may wish to build up the compost on one side to give a more natural, undulating effect. Use a tamper, which may be a cotton reel on a cane handle, to firm down and compact the compost.

Start planting at the outside of the container and work towards the middle. You know that there will be adequate space left for the central plants because you have already worked out the spacing on your paper plan.

Shake each plant from its pot and, if there is space to admit it through the neck of the container, keep the soil ball around the roots intact. If not, gently knock off the soil without damaging the roots. Scoop out a shallow hole in the compost with your fingers or an extended spoon as appropriate and lower the plant into place. In a bottle garden you may choose to grip the plant between a spoon and fork, or to spear the stem between the tines of the fork. If you do this you may need to use another tool to ease the plant away from the fork prongs.

In a very narrow-necked container – a wine bottle, for example – you will simply have to push the plant gently through the neck, root first, then ease the leaves through as carefully as possible. It may be helpful to wrap the leaves in a strip of paper or polythene to form a narrow, protective tube and to push them through in this way. Hold one edge of the tube so that you can pull it back through the neck once the leaves have been released. Trying to retrieve a piece of plastic or paper that has sprung into a wide, unwieldy shape can be exasperating.

After inserting each plant, scrape back the compost to cover the roots and firm it down

RIGHT Cut a piece of polythene or paper and wrap it, tube style, around the plant. Gently lower the plant through the aperture. Hold on to a corner of the plastic so that you can easily withdraw it. Use an extended tamping stick, a cotton reel on a cane, to firm in the plant.

LEFT A needle or sharp implement mounted on a cane is useful for pushing wayward stems into place and for spearing fallen leaves.

around them with your fingers or a tamper. If any roots remain exposed, add a little more compost to cover them.

Once you have planted the terrarium, clean the inside of the glass with a piece of damp sponge or small cosmetic brush. No matter how careful you have been and how effective your use of a paper cone or funnel, some compost particles seem invariably to cling to the inner surface of the container.

WATERING

Planting a terrarium may be considered the artistic stage of the operation. When it comes to watering the plants, however, science takes over. Achieving the correct moisture balance, especially in a sealed container, is by far the most important single factor and the one that, literally, is a matter of life or death to the plants. It cannot be stated too frequently that over-watering an indoor garden, or even a single indoor plant, is the most likely cause of disappointment. One may think of it as killing the plants with kindness, but kill them it certainly will.

In the normal course of events and when the moisture balance is correct, a terrarium will show the greatest amount of condensation in the early morning, when the outside temperature is at its lowest. The low temperature causes the moisture in the enclosed atmosphere inside the container to condense on the cold glass, but it should clear gradually as the outside temperature rises.

RIGHT A small cosmetic brush on a cane can be used to brush away loose, dry compost from the inside of the glass.

THE RAIN CYCLE

If a terrarium is correctly balanced it imitates the pattern of the rain cycle. The plants take in moisture from the compost through their roots and give it off in the form of vapour through their leaves. This vapour collects on the inside of the glass in the form of condensation, trickles down and is reabsorbed by the compost, keeping it moist but not wet. (As we have seen, plastic domes and containers react in a slightly different way, and condensation tends to adhere to the surface and may then drip down vertically.) There should be only enough moisture in the container to nurture the plants and effect this natural cycle. Any more, and the plants' roots will be permanently waterlogged.

→ **moisture**
– – → **evaporated moisture**
○○○ **condensation**

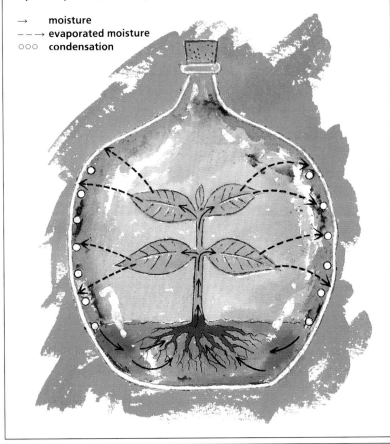

To achieve this all-important balance it is best to add water little by little initially and to check the terrarium each day to assess the level of condensation. You can always add more water as and when you judge it to be necessary, but removing excess water is a problem. You can add water either by trickling it down the inside of the glass, which will help to clean it, or by spraying it evenly over the plants, using a fine mist spray. Leave the container overnight and check the condensation that has formed.

If there is none, particularly in a sealed container, the chances are that the compost is too dry and a little more water is needed. Add some water sparingly, and check again on the following day. Add a little more water if still no condensation has formed.

If, on the other hand, there is a heavy layer of condensation inside the glass, and this does not clear during the morning, it is likely that the initial watering was over-generous. Remove as much of the condensed moisture as you can with a dry cloth or, in a narrow-necked container, a piece of dry sponge on a wire, and leave the container open to allow as much evaporation as possible to take place. Leave open one panel of a leaded terrarium, remove the stopper of a carboy or other bottle, or move the covering of an aquarium slightly to one side. Remember to make sure that a heavy glass lid is safe, especially if children or animals might knock into it. Check the condensation level again the following day and clear the glass again if it is still heavily misted, so that the moisture does not drip or trickle back into the compost.

MAINTENANCE

Day-to-day observation will show you when the moisture balance in a terrarium is just right, when some condensation forms inside the container on most days, and the plants look healthy. Remember that plants in wide-open glass containers – fruit bowls and mixing bowls, for example – will need regular watering during the growing season, but you must not allow the compost to become wet.

Once this balance is achieved, your indoor garden should need only the minimum of after-care. Remove any leaves that start to discolour before they become diseased and can infect others. Snip off any unruly stems or too vigorous shoots that press against the glass and remove flowers as soon as they begin to fade.

If you choose to include flowering plants in your display or to feature a single plant in, say, a brandy snifter, you may consider these as expendable, and rest or even discard them as soon as the flowering season is over. Only the most ardent admirers of, say, the African violet would consider it the perfect table decoration once the clusters of pink, white, mauve, blue or red flowers had become little more than a fond memory.

ABOVE Reminiscent of the Wardian cases that were used to transport plants during overseas expeditions, this beautifully constructed leaded terrarium gives an opportunity for "landscaping" and imaginative planting.

LEFT The pretty pink-splashed polka-dot plant *(Hypoestes sanguinolenta)* needs some sunshine to maintain its leaf colour. It is featured in this terrarium with a variegated ivy *(Hedera helix)*, two maidenhair ferns *(Adiantum)*, a green-and-yellow-leaved, slow-growing Japanese spindle *(Euonymus japonicus "Microphyllus")* and a selaginella.

Fern and Moss Garden

Tropical-looking ferns and dense mosses feature in this terrarium, while colour contrast is provided by a pink-leaved tradescantia.

YOU WILL NEED

- terrarium
- washed gravel or pea gravel
- charcoal, broken into small pieces
- peat-based compost
- small trowel
- plants such as maidenhair fern (*Adiantum raddianum*), Cretan brake fern (*Pteris cretica*),
- button fern (*Pellaea rotundifolia*), creeping moss (*Selaginella*), and a variegated form of the flowering inch plant (*Tradescantia cerinthoides* syn. *T. blossfeldiana*)
- tamping stick
- water spray
- small piece of wet sponge

1 A shallow layer of gravel to facilitate drainage is covered with a thin layer of broken charcoal.

2 The depth of compost will depend on the size of the plants and their roots. In a container of this size a layer of about 7.5cm/3in is usually adequate.

3 It is easiest to begin planting from the outside of the container with the low-growing mosses and creeping ferns.

4 It is important to firm in all the plants, using your fingers or a tamping stick. Roots must have a firm hold on the compost if the plants are to flourish.

5 Watering should be sparing at first until the balance can be assessed after one or even two days. The spray will also help to clean the inside of the glass.

6 A small piece of natural or plastic sponge is useful for removing any soil particles clinging to the inside of the glass.

7 The pinky leaves of the tradescantia contrast strikingly with the light and dark greens of the ferns and mosses. A spotlight beamed on the group shows it to its best advantage.

A Traditional Bottle Garden

A green glass bottle garden, which will enhance the appeal of the flora, needs to be placed in a bright situation to compensate for the diminution of natural light.

YOU WILL NEED

- glass bottle garden or carboy
- paper cone or funnel
- washed gravel or pea gravel
- charcoal, broken into small pieces
- peat-based compost
- large spoon or trowel
- paper pattern of bottle dimension
- plants such as spider plant (*Chlorophytum comosum*), parlour palm (*Chamaedorea elegans* syn. *Neanthe bella*), Madagascar dragon tree (*Dracaena marginata*), creeping moss (*Selaginella*) and a Mediterranean fern (*Pteris vittata*)
- spoon, fork, cotton reel and spike bound on to canes
- sponge mounted on flexible wire

1 A paper cone will help to direct the gravel, charcoal and compost into even layers on the base of the bottle.

2 The extended spoon and fork are used as a pair of tongs to insert the plants, in this case a creeping moss.

3 A cotton reel on a length of cane makes an effective tamping stick to firm the compost around the plants' roots.

4 However careful you are when planting the garden, some compost or loose leaves will almost certainly adhere to the inside of the glass. Remove them with a piece of sponge on a wire before or after watering.

5 The contrasting textures and leaf colours of the fern and the creeping moss can be seen to advantage in a close-up view of the planted bottle garden. With the sunlight slanting through the green glass of the bottle garden, you can enjoy the added effect of the coloured pattern reflected, stained-glass-window style, on the wall beside it.

A Modern Version

Just to prove that an elegant terrarium need be neither leaded nor bottle shaped, we have chosen a modern vase with a petal-shaped top. A cork disc could be used to create a sealed environment.

YOU WILL NEED

- bulbous glass vase
- paper cone or funnel
- washed gravel or pea gravel
- charcoal, broken into small pieces
- peat-based compost
- large spoon or trowel
- spoon, fork, cotton reel and spike bound on to canes
- sponge mounted on flexible wire
- paper pattern of the vase dimension
- plants such as a Mediterranean fern *(Pteris vittata)*, creeping peperomia *(Peperomia prostrata)* and polka-dot plant *(Hypoestes sanguinolenta)*

1 With the gravel, charcoal and compost in place, directed around the base by means of a cone, holes to receive each plant are made with the extended spoon. The plants are held between the spoon and fork so that they can be lowered through the aperture.

2 The flexibility of the wire – compared to the rigidity of a length of cane – allows it to be used all around the inside of the glass for cleaning and demisting.

3 The light filtered through a macramé curtain is both flattering and beneficial to the planted garden. The choice of background can significantly change the perception of the group.

A Modern Bell-jar

It may be difficult to obtain an original 18th-century bell-jar, but you can emulate the principle by using a modern dome, originally designed to be used as a food cover.

1 Put the cover in position several times as you proceed with the planting. If one plant has unacceptably long or trailing stems that cannot be accommodated, cut them off at this stage.

YOU WILL NEED

- glass dome and base, such as a cheese dish; ours was 20cm/8in across
- waterproof lining dish; we used an old baking tin
- washed gravel or pea gravel
- charcoal, broken into small pieces
- peat-based compost
- spoon or trowel
- tamping stick
- scissors or florist's scissors

- water spray
- plants such as polka-dot plant (*Hypoestes sanguinolenta*), silver vine (*Epipremnum pictum* "Argyraeus" syn. *Scindapsus pictus* "Argyraeus"), a dwarf creeping fig (*Ficus pumila* "Minima") and button fern (*Pellaea rotundifolia*)

2 This group, in its own enclosed environment, is ideally suited for display in a bathroom where it will be unaffected by the varying humidity.

Child's Candy Jar Garden

A large glass candy jar or its plastic equivalent can be put to decorative use as a horizontal or vertical planter. A give-away plastic jar is ideal for a child's first attempt at indoor gardening.

YOU WILL NEED

- large candy jar
- washed gravel or pea gravel
- charcoal, broken into small pieces
- peat-based compost
- large spoon
- plants such as polka-dot plant (*Hypoestes*

sanguinolenta), a variegated ivy (*Hedera helix*) and a variegated form of the flowering inch plant (*Tradescantia cerinthoides* syn. *T. blossfeldiana*)
- sharp implement mounted on a cane

1 Lay the jar on its side and insert the layers of gravel and charcoal. The compost can then be spooned over the charcoal to make an even layer about 5cm/2in deep.

2 Firmly plant the tradescantia about one-third of the way from the end of the jar, spreading out its stems to cover the jar's length.

3 With the polka-dot plant and ivy in place, use a sharp implement to arrange the stems so that they are not bent, crushed or obscured by one another.

4 After watering and with the lid in place, the jar can become part of a display on a bright windowsill or toy box.

In the Limelight

A simple but elegant terrarium like this looks equally at home in a rustic or a formal setting. All the plants are popular and readily available.

Against a dark background but with the winter sunshine illuminating the plants, the terrarium looks well in a countrified setting.

YOU WILL NEED

- leaded terrarium
- washed gravel or pea gravel
- charcoal, broken into small pieces
- small trowel
- tamping stick
- plants such as creeping moss (Selaginella), maidenhair fern

(Adiantum raddianum), variegated ivy (Hedera helix) and a variegated flowering inch plant (Tradescantia fluminensis "Albovittata" syn. albiflora "Albovittata")

The terrarium works equally well in a more formal setting against a heavily textured wallcovering that picks out the pink tones of the tradescantia.

CHAPTER THREE

A Case for Orchids

Orchids have a special place in the hearts and minds of indoor gardeners. Some people so admire the exotic shapes and colours of the blooms and appreciate their unusually long-lasting properties that they are prepared to go to any lengths to create the ideal conditions for them, even stretching the household budget to provide a little extra heat. Other indoor gardeners, swayed by tales of the plants' impossible demands and unaware of the varied requirements of the different genera, never even try to grow them. These are the people who do not know what they are missing!

Most orchids are native to the tropical regions of the Far East and South America, yet they are surprisingly adaptable in terms of indoor habitat. Some of the more popular genera will flourish in temperatures of 18–30°C/64–86°F during the day and 10–16°C/50–61°F at night, temperatures not far removed from the levels maintained in many homes. They do have specific needs in terms of humidity, however, and cannot tolerate the hot, dry conditions that are found in well-insulated, centrally heated rooms. To grow orchids in an open container, raise the localized humidity level by placing the dish in a larger outer one spread with a layer of gravel or small stones that are kept permanently moist. Alternatively, place a purpose-made humidifier close to the plants.

Many keen amateur growers raise their plants in an orchid case – a terrarium by another name. Some cases are elaborate constructions with glass on three sides, a natural-looking fibreglass "rock face" lining at the rear, in imitation of the plants' natural habitat, and heating and lighting elements so that the temperature and duration of the light can be controlled. That degree of sophistication may be the ideal and long-term aspiration of new

enthusiasts, but as long as a few simple guidelines are followed, it is possible to grow orchids successfully in an "ordinary" terrarium.

As you can see from the recommendations for each genus, the minimum temperature requirements vary within a small margin (although slight transgressions are not likely to prove disastrous) and cool nights are important. The maximum recommended temperature is constant for them all and should never exceed 30°C/86°F. Other conditions to be avoided are strong, direct sunshine – high noon in summer – direct artificial heat from radiators or fires and draughts. Growing the plants in a terrarium obviates this last hazard.

LIGHT

Orchids thrive on some direct sunshine, although they should never be placed in the full glare of the summer sun. Ideally, they should be given the benefit of a south-facing situation in winter and be moved close to an east- or west-facing window in summer. If this is not possible, the equivalent intensity of artificial light is a satisfactory substitute. They need a total of 10–15 hours of light each day during the growing season.

WATER

It may not be possible to recreate precisely the natural growing conditions of orchids in the wild where, as epiphytes, they grow not in soil but with their roots wrapped around tree branches. This means that rainwater washes over the roots and quickly drains away – a clue to the plants' preferred watering programme

LEFT A tall, narrow terrarium is planted with coral and cream *Cymbidium* orchids, which make an elegant and stylish group.

ABOVE An example of *Cattleya*, known as the corsage orchid, which needs a constant temperature and high humidity.

when they are grown in the home. It is advisable to plant them in a specially coarse and quick-draining compost, or in a medium made of, for example, chopped pine bark. Garden centres and specialist shops sell various types that are suitable.

In imitation of their natural moisture source, use tepid rainwater or, if that is not available, soft water; leave it to stand overnight at room temperature if you have brought in icy-cold water from the garden. When orchids are grown in open containers, water them sparingly when the compost or culture has thoroughly dried out. The roots need to be able to take in air between waterings. Those grown in an enclosed container should need only very occasional watering. The top or opening should be removed from time to time to facilitate ventilation.

FEEDING

Orchids grown in dish gardens benefit from occasional feeding during the growing period, but never continue to feed those genera that need a winter rest. A liquid fertilizer used at half the normally recommended dilution may be applied with every second or third watering.

MAINTENANCE

In order to achieve an extended display of flowers, you might like to consider rotating the plants in a terrarium, replacing one as it reaches the end of its flowering season with another that is just coming into bloom. It is easier to do this if you leave the orchids in their pots when you place them in the terrarium, just covering the tops with compost if you want to give a "planted" appearance.

Cattleya

These corsage orchids, as they are aptly named, are ideal for growing in a terrarium since they need a constant temperature and a high humidity. The waxy flowers may be 10–15cm/ 4–6in across.

LEFT Seen through the clear glass of the terrarium, a cream-coloured *Cymbidium* orchid, which should flower for several weeks.

ABOVE The popular slipper orchid, *Paphiopedilum*, has a pouch-shaped lower lip.

RIGHT The *Odontoglossum*, or tiger orchid, must have a long period of winter rest.

Cymbidium

Coming mainly from the Himalayas, the *Cymbidium* genus can tolerate a minimum winter temperature of 10°C/50°F. It has the common name of boat orchid, which is thought to derive from the distinctively curved shape of the lower petal or lip. There are two types: the miniatures, which are perfectly suited to a small dish garden or terrarium and which bear flowers about 4cm/1½in across; and standards, which may reach a stem height of 45cm/18in.

Miltonia

The species in this genus, which come mainly from Brazil and Colombia, have rounded, somewhat flattened flowers, a characteristic that gives rise to the popular name of pansy orchid. Miltonia orchids require a minimum temperature of 13°C/55°F and dislike temperature changes. They are in the medium size range.

Odontoglossum

Aim for a minimum temperature of 13°C/55°F for species in this genus, which originated in high-altitude regions of tropical South and Central America and is sometimes called princess of the Andes or tiger orchid. Winter rest is essential.

Paphiopedilum

A minimum temperature of 13°C/55°F is preferable for these orchids, which are known as ladies' slipper orchids or slipper orchids and are sometimes listed as *Cypripedium*. They are native to southeast Asia, can tolerate a slightly lower intensity of light than other orchids and need little or no rest period in winter. The flowers, which may be up to 10cm/4in across, have a pouched-shaped lower petal or lip, and the foliage may be striped or mottled.

Phalaenopsis

These moth orchids, as they are known, derive from southeast Asia and have been bred to have a compact growth habit and long flowering period. Unlike some other genera, they need little or no rest in winter. Their preferred minimum temperature is 13°C/55°F, but this is not critical.

BELOW *Phalaenopsis*, the moth orchid, has a compact growth habit and long flowering period.

CHAPTER FOUR

Choosing and Planting a Dish Garden

ish gardens offer a wealth of opportunities for interior garden design. They can vary in shape and complexity from a simple saucer garden that a child might plant to a miniature Japanese garden complete with paths, a replica bridge and pagoda, and include all the shapes and sizes in between.

The containers used tend to be plain and unobtrusive, so that they do not detract from the colour and decorative aspects of the plants and any accessories included in the design. They usually have drainage holes, which means that they should not be placed on polished wood or any other surface that could be stained by moisture seepage or condensation. If you do wish to stand a dish garden on an unprotected surface, you could place it on a tray or other waterproof stand, the equivalent of using a cache-pot or jardinière to cover plant pots.

The alternative is to use a container that does not have holes and to line it with efficient drainage materials of the kind used in a

LIVING STONES

ithops or living stones will make an attractive display in a dish garden. There are several different species to choose from, and they bear surprisingly large, daisy-like flowers in a variety of colours. They will do best near a sunny window, but they need to be kept cool and dry during the winter dormancy period.

BELOW LEFT Casseroles, baking dishes, jelly moulds, decorative pots and even ashtrays, as well as a purpose-made pottery planter, can be used for indoor displays of cacti, succulents, alpines and other plants.

BELOW Taking a broad view of the term dish garden, wooden trugs, baskets and woven trays can all be used as decorative containers if they are provided with a waterproof lining.

terrarium. A thin layer of pea gravel and another of horticultural charcoal, aquarium filter charcoal or broken up barbecue charcoal, coupled with meagre watering, should keep the plants healthy and prevent them from becoming waterlogged.

You will find a variety of suitable planters in garden centres and other specialist garden shops. Styles range from heavy glazed and unglazed earthenware examples to plastic look-alikes and those that are, uncompromisingly, shiny plastic. Small potteries are good sources of planters, too, and you may find sturdy examples of hand-made pottery dishes purpose-made for planting. The one shown in the project later on in this chapter is raised on a shallow platform and has two drainage holes.

Other fruitful hunting-grounds are boot sales, junk shops and street markets, where you may find real planters or a selection of household items that could be adapted to the purpose. Any shallow dish, oval or round, square or

rectangular, may be suitable. You may also consider using a small stone or slate sink, glazed or unglazed pottery baking and serving dishes, casseroles, chicken and fish bricks (you need only one of the halves for planting) and pottery jelly moulds. Even a container that seems suitable in every way except for the fact that it is damaged can be used – grow a trailing plant such as a miniature ivy or tradescantia so that it masks the fault.

If you are prepared not to take the "dish" element of the term dish garden literally, you could also add decorative tins and shallow baskets to the list of potential containers. Line a basket or shallow woven bowl with thick polythene to make it waterproof, then you can add the drainage material and compost and plant it in the usual way. Indeed, baskets and growing plants have a particular affinity, and you can create a variety of pleasing styles using old woven willow, split cane and rush specimens.

ABOVE A deeply ridged and scalloped shell makes an unusual plant container. As it has no holes, a shallow layer of gravel and charcoal beneath the soil is essential. Planted with a spectacular variegated ivy (*Hedera helix*), the group is appropriate for a bathroom setting. Smaller shells of varied shapes are pressed into the soil to add to the marine appearance.

CHOOSING THE PLANTS

Without perhaps going to the lengths of creating an indoor garden that will resemble a "willow pattern" scene, you can compose gardens with a variety of themes. You may like to create a scented garden, planting a selection of herbs in the spring, or a silver and white garden, which would have a cool, sophisticated look reminiscent of a silver garden border. With so many flowering plants to choose from, you could compose gardens that would coordinate with the decor of your living-room, bedroom or kitchen, and you could change the flowers from season to season as the colours fade. You might

decide to go for a tropical look and plant a dish garden with a selection of cacti, or you might prefer to create your own version of an oasis with a range of fleshy-leaved succulents. If you wanted a more romantic effect with the kind of garden beloved by children, you might take a cue from the nursery rhyme and plant a garden of "silver bells and cockle shells" that shimmers with the iridescence of shells used as accessories between the plants.

Whatever your personal preferences, the main thing to remember when you design a dish garden is that the plants you choose must be compatible. They will be planted in the same container, enjoy the same drainage and growing

LEFT **Planted in a green-glazed casserole dish, a group of desert cacti and other succulents makes an interesting study in shape and texture. Centre of attention is the red-domed Hibotan cactus (*Gymnocalycium mihanovichii* var. *hibotan*). The two columnar cacti are from the *Cereus* genus, and the two random-shaped ones are opuntias. The bunny ears cactus (*Opuntia microdasys*) has particularly intrusive spikes. The round ball shape is a golden barrel cactus (*Echinocactus grusonii*). The succulents are the panda plant (*Kalanchoë tomentosa*), blue echeveria (*Echeveria glauca*) and a cotyledon.**

media, and be subject to the same watering programme and a similar degree of light and heat. It is important to bear this in mind before you buy any of the plants. Assess the conditions you are able to offer – few of us are inclined to heat our homes specifically for the benefit of the plants – and make your selection accordingly. Having decided on an appropriate range of plants, do not allow yourself then to be tempted to add, say, one shade-loving plant to a group that thrives on full sun. Such a move is not fair to the plant – or to yourself as a gardener.

As a general rule, a dish garden looks most attractive when the plants span, within the confines of the container, a range of heights, shapes and leaf colours. It can be effective to choose one plant with a tall, erect form, which towers above the others, some that are compact and bushy, and at least one that has a trailing habit and softens the hard outline of the container. Ivies and tradescantias, among many others, fulfil this role admirably.

If you wish to plant a long-lasting scented garden, you could choose some evergreen herbs, adding just one or two annuals if you want colour and leaf contrast. A small bay or rosemary, which you would have to prune, sage and purple sage, thyme and golden thyme would all be appropriate. You could add a small

clump of chives for the contrasting shape of their grass-like leaves, and a scented geranium for the sweetness of its aroma. Choose from, among others, *Pelargonium crispum minor*, which is lemon-scented; *P. odoratissimum*, which is reminiscent of oak leaves; the rose-scented P. *graveolens* and perhaps the most pungent of all, P. *tomentosum*, which smells of peppermint.

If you want a silver-leaved garden, when contrasting leaf colour is less of an option, it is especially important to achieve an interesting balance of plant height and shape, and of leaf shape and texture. An attractive choice would be a silver-green mint geranium (*Pelargonium tomentosum*), which should bear small clusters of

pale pink flowers in early summer, and two or three white-flowering pinks (*Dianthus*), which are often not considered as house plants but which do well in cool, dry conditions. For the trailing element you could include a variegated ivy, pinching out the growing tips two or three times a year to keep it in proportion with the container.

Cacti

The subject of cacti cultivation is almost a life-long study in itself since there are so many possible permutations of size and shape, texture and flower colours. There are two main types of cacti, which are native to different natural habitats and which have, therefore, differing cultural requirements.

By far the larger group are desert cacti, which come from the warm, semi-desert regions of America. These cacti require as much sunshine as possible, especially during the flowering season, and are therefore well suited to south-facing windowsills. Desert cacti need very little or no water between mid-autumn and early spring, a lack of requirement which can impose a serious strain on an inexperienced gardener anxious to wield the indoor watering can at regular intervals.

The second group is made up of forest cacti whose natural home is the forest regions of tropical America, where they grow as epiphytes on trees. Forest cacti are easily recognized by their trailing habit and flattened, leaf-like stems. They are suitable for north- and east-facing windowsills, since they require some shade during the hottest months of the year. They may need a little water and some feeding in winter.

Although a cactus garden is among the easiest to maintain, it is a popular fallacy that the plants will thrive and even flower in sandy

LEFT A centuries-old flower pot is an unusual container for a quartet of cacti, but the sandy, earthy textures and colour are in perfect harmony. The cactus in flower is *Parodia sanguiniflora*; the others are an *Opuntia microdasys* var. *albispina*, a column cactus *(Cereus peruvianus)* and an *Opuntia cylindrica*.

LEFT A green glazed casserole with a chubby handle makes an interesting, asymmetrical container for a selection of succulents. The red-flowering *Kalanchoë blossfeldiana* is the colour highlight among the tooth-leaved *Aloe variegata*, the tree-like propeller plant (*Crassula falcata*), the taller silver jade plant (*Crassula arborescens*) with its red-edged leaves and the curving and variegated elephant bush (*Portulacaria afra*).

soil and direct heat with no moisture. As with plants of all kinds, cacti need the right conditions for them if they are to reach their full decorative potential. By careful selection of the plants, and attention to their minimal but specific requirements, it is possible to plant a dish garden which will display some flowers almost all the year round. It is worth noting, for the impatient among us, that most cacti will flower only on new growth, and that about half the varieties can be expected to flower indoors in the third or fourth year.

Succulents

Cacti, with their exotic desert-bloom associations, are a distinct group of succulents and, with two or three exceptions, are leafless. What they lack in leaves they make up for in the bristly cushions called areoles, and in spines, needles, hooks and hairs. Other succulents, defined as plants with fleshy leaves or stems that can store water, offer equally broad scope for dish-garden design, and can be as weird and wonderful, as compact or spreading, as you choose.

Most succulents are native to dry regions of the world and so have common environmental needs. Their general requirements are sunshine, fresh air, a free-draining compost, water in the growing season and a cold and dry resting period in the winter. To bring them to their full potential and to encourage flowering for a number of years, winter dormancy is essential, and an outdoor "holiday" in the summer is highly recommended. It is a good idea to take all but the largest dish gardens – some sink gardens may be too heavy to move – on to a balcony or into the garden for several sunny days during the summer. If this is not possible, then at least open the windows so that the succulents can, literally, take a breath of fresh air.

Bromeliads

Still with an eye to exotic-looking dish gardens, bromeliads are yet another option and one that perhaps presents the indoor gardener with something more of a challenge. These plants are native to the American jungles, where they flourish on the forest floor or among the orchids in the trees. Some bromeliads are grown specifically for the beauty of their foliage, which can vary from the bright red of *Aechmea* "Foster's Favorite", known as lacquered wine cup, through the red, green and yellow striped rainbow star (*Cryptanthus bromelioides* var. *tricolor*), to the tiger-striped appearance of *Cryptanthus zonatus*. Others, such as the blue-flowered torch (*Tillandsia lindenii*), queen's tears (*Billbergia nutans*) and *Guzmania lingulata*, are grown for their showy flowers which, although slow to appear (some species take several years to reach the flowering stage), may last several months.

Most bromeliads require a brightly lit situation, but do not place them in full sun – a south-facing windowsill is not suitable. Foliage species do well in an average temperature of about 10°C/50°F but 23°C/74°F or more may be required to bring flowering plants into bloom. Bromeliads require good drainage and only moderate watering. The actual method of watering is one of the unusual characteristics of the plants – you pour it into the central cup or "vase" formed by the leaves rather than into the compost. The plants may be watered and fed through their leaves in summer, using diluted liquid fertilizer.

Have ready everything you will need before you start planting a dish garden – the container, the drainage material, some peat-based compost, a planting plan, plants and your tools. With the easy access that these shallow, open containers afford, standard tools such as a dibber and an indoor trowel and fork are all that should be needed. Add any accessories you plan to include – small rocks, stones, fossils and shells, for example – and an indoor watering-can, and you are all set to begin.

If your container has no drainage holes, spread a thin layer of a drainage material such as washed gravel or coarse grit, and then a layer of small pieces of charcoal to act as a filter. Next add a layer of a peat-based compost. Use potting compost, **not** seed compost. Firm it down with your fist, a piece of stone or a small piece of wood.

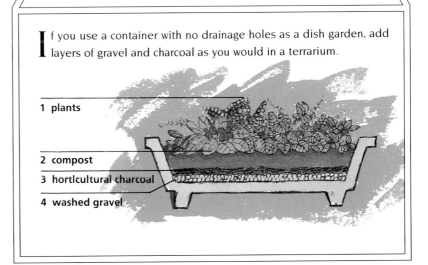

CROSS SECTION OF A DISH GARDEN

If you use a container with no drainage holes as a dish garden, add layers of gravel and charcoal as you would in a terrarium.

1 plants
2 compost
3 horticultural charcoal
4 washed gravel

LEFT A small, rough dish with a pebbly interior is perfect for a child's "saucer garden". A scattering of gravel and charcoal beneath the soil facilitates drainage.

Arrange your plants on a piece of paper cut to the size of the container base. Make sure that a tall, wide-spreading plant does not obscure a smaller, low-growing one (and rob it of light) and that the tallest, straightest plant does not look "all stalk". If it does and all its foliage is clustered at the top, plant a medium-height specimen close to it to enhance the interest and disguise the stalk.

Begin by planting the tallest feature plant and continue clockwise until the dish is complete. Scoop away just enough compost to make space for the roots and soil ball. Tip the plant gently from the pot, cupping the roots in one hand. Firm the roots into the compost with your fingers, scrape back the disturbed compost and firm it around the stem. Snip off any damaged leaves. Add a little water so that the compost is moist but not wet.

Position any accessories such as shells and rocks so that they separate the plants and help to emphasize their decorative features. A trailing succulent winding its way over a piece of jagged rock may look far more dramatic than it would if it were seen next to another fleshy green plant or against the surface of the compost. A collection of alpine species may look more natural if a few stones are placed here and there on the compost, and small flowering plants will look all the prettier for the addition of pearly pink, grey, brown, white or coral shells.

Keep your dish garden evenly and sparingly watered during the growing season and be prepared to move it away from full sun or a frosty windowsill according to the plants' needs. Remove any discoloured or fading leaves and flowers, and prune any shoots that are too vigorous for their surroundings. Apart from that, there is nothing to do but admire your handiwork and enjoy watching your dish garden grow!

RIGHT In winter it is an aromatic study in greens, all the greens from nearly yellow to almost grey. The deep woven basket is first lined with polythene, then drainage layers of gravel and charcoal are added. The plants are a golden-leaved form of feverfew (Chrysanthemum parthenium "Aureum"), tricolour and purple sage (Salvia officinalis), a dwarf blue-flowering lavender (Lavandula angustifolia "Munstead"), garlic chives or Chinese chives (Allium tuberosum) and three sweetly scented thymes, the golden variety (Thymus × citriodorus "Aureus"), broad-leaved thyme (T. pulegioides) and a variegated thyme (T. × citriodorus).

All Squared Up

A square, hand-made pottery planter makes a rather oriental-style container for a collection of succulents, which have been chosen for the variety of their leaf colour.

YOU WILL NEED

- square, shallow pottery planter; ours was 25cm/10in across
- washed gravel or pea gravel
- charcoal, broken into small pieces
- loam-based compost
- spoon or small trowel
- tamping stick
- cacti and other succulents such as *Opuntia sublata*, silver jade plant

(*Crassula arborescens*), *C. conjuncta*, crown of thorns (*Euphorbia milii* var. *splendens*), South American air plant (*Kalanchoë fedtschenkoi*), candle plant (*Senecio articulatus* syn. *Kleinia articulata*), elephant bush (*Portulacaria afra*) and golden sedum (*Sedum adolphii*)

1 The dish is planted to be viewed mainly from three sides, so the tallest succulents are grouped together, tree like, towards the back. The sedums are planted so that they trail over the rim of the container, breaking up the straight lines. It is important to firm in all the shallow-rooted plants with a tamping stick.

2 A background of a muted colour, such as grey-green, brown or cream, flatters plants that were selected for the subtle variety of leaf colour. In this group the colour ranges from pale cream, grey-green and sharp green to a tinge of red.

Silver-leaved Gift Bowl

Silver-leaved plants, with the promise of flowers to come, would make an appropriate gift for a silver wedding anniversary or to mark a christening.

YOU WILL NEED

- pottery dish; ours was 23cm/9in in diameter
- washed gravel or pea gravel
- charcoal, broken into small pieces
- peat-based or similar compost
- alpine grit (optional)
- spoon or small trowel
- tamping stick
- silver-leaved plants such as cotton lavender

(Santolina neapolitana), a purple-blue-flowering lavender *(Lavandula angustifolia* "Hidcote"), mauve-flowering *Erinus alpinus* and white-flowering *Leucanthemum hosmariense* (syn. *Chrysanthemum hosmariense)*
- decorative shells

1 Spread a thin layer of gravel and then of charcoal in the dish and add the compost. Make a hole for each plant, scrape the soil back to cover the roots and firm them in with the tamping stick.

2 When all the plants are firmed in, you may, if you wish, cover the soil with a scattering of alpine grit. We added a few decorative shells to form a textured background to the plants.

3 A wrapping of printed transparent paper and a generous bow of silver and white ribbon transform the planted bowl into a celebratory gift.

Herb Basket

A wooden garden trug is filled with aromatic plants, many of them culinary herbs. An alternative version of the planting will add a splash of vibrant colour.

YOU WILL NEED

- wooden trug or deep basket; ours was 25cm/10in long
- piece of polythene as liner
- washed gravel or pea gravel
- charcoal, broken into small pieces
- peat-based compost
- spoon or small trowel
- tamping stick
- scissors
- aromatic plants

such as lavender (*Lavandula angustifolia*), rosemary (*Rosmarinus officinalis*), thyme (*Thymus vulgaris*) and sweet marjoram (*Origanum majorana*); the flowering nasturtium plants (*Tropaeolum majus*) are optional extras

1 Line the base and sides of the trug with polythene and trim the edges. Spoon in a shallow layer of gravel and cover it with the charcoal.

2 Add the compost and firm the surface to compact it. Make a hole in the compost large enough to take each plant complete with the soil around its root ball.

3 When you have positioned each plant and scraped the compost back over its roots, firm it down with a tamping stick.

4 A herb basket is a portable indoor garden and you can move it from place to place so that the plants can benefit from strong light or sunshine. The group is especially suited to a kitchen.

To add a splash of colour after the spring-and-summer flowering herbs have finished blooming, you can add two or three trailing nasturtium plants.

Desert Brown

Use a sandy-brown baking dish and you can make believe the cacti are grouped around an oasis! At this stage, when it is the only one in flower, the focal point of the group is the powder-puff cactus.

1 Carefully ease the cactus out of the pot, keeping as much compost as possible around the roots. The compost is mixed with polystyrene granules to aid drainage and aeration. Position the plants well apart so that each one may be viewed individually and appreciated for its distinctive characteristics.

YOU WILL NEED

- oval baking dish; ours was 30cm/12in long
- washed gravel or pea gravel
- charcoal, broken into small pieces
- loam-based compost
- spoon or trowel
- tamping stick
- cacti and other succulents such as the powder-puff

cactus (*Mammillaria bocasana*), lace cactus (*M. elongata*), bunny ears cactus (*Opuntia microdasys*), peanut cactus (*Chamaecereus silvestri*) and *Astrophytum, Aloe* and *Euphorbia*
- stones or pebbles

2 This group of plants prefers a position in sun and shade in summer. Accessories such as craggy stones or pebbles are in keeping with the nature of the collection.

CHAPTER FIVE

Siting and Lighting

hoosing a situation for your bottle garden or dish garden is not simply a question of aesthetics, of deciding where it would look best or which corner of the room would be most enhanced by the display. It is, rather, a question of how much light and heat the specific plants need and where in the home those requirements can most nearly be met.

We say most nearly met, because it has to be admitted that not many homes offer the ideal growing conditions for plants that may have originated in a desert, a jungle or a region characterized by a warm, constant temperature. If plants could choose their own environment, it would not be a living-room in which the humidity is low, the light is medium to poor and the day and night temperatures are subject to wide fluctuations. Moreover, many house plants have to undergo the initial shock of being suddenly transferred from ideal nursery conditions provided by a well-lit and humid commercial glasshouse to domestic situations only moderately suited to their needs. The first few days in their new surroundings can be a testing time for plants and growers alike!

It is common knowledge that, to ensure healthy growth, all plants, even ferns and other known shade-lovers, need some light. The question is, how much? The details in the Directory at the end of this book will tell you which plants do best in bright light, in partial shade or in shade, and this should help you to make your initial choice. It is courting disaster, or at least disappointment, to select a range of plants, tradescantias for example, that need bright light and even some direct sunlight if your chosen site is a table a couple of paces away from a north-facing window.

That short distance from a window can make all the difference to the quality and intensity of the light and thus the suitability of a situation

for a bottle garden or a dish garden. It is difficult to appreciate just how much and how quickly light diminishes within a room as you move away from a window because the human eye has the ability to adjust to changing light values without our being aware of them. You could make your own assessment of how light fades by carrying out a simple experiment with a

ABOVE By placing the planted garden in front of a macramé curtain the light is filtered and therefore less harsh on the garden.

LIGHT

Because our eyes accommodate so quickly to differences in the intensity of light, it is only by using something as precise as a photographic light meter that we are able to judge the differences that can exist within a room just a short distance from, say, a window. In general terms, plants that flourish in bright light, such as cacti and other succulents, may be placed on or close to a south-facing windowsill. However, few plants can withstand the effect of full sun on glass and in mid-summer you should provide partial shading or move the plants out of direct light.

direct light   **shade**   **partial shade**

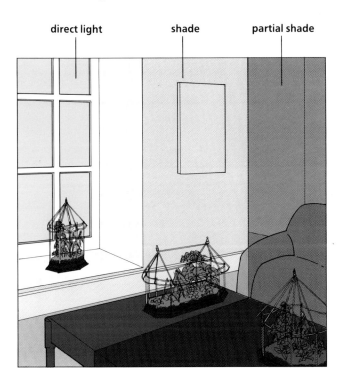

photographic light meter. Measure the light in front of the window, beside it, half-way into the room and in a corner of the room. You will be surprised at the variation you will record.

Plants that do well in some direct sunlight, such as African violets (*Saintpaulia*), ornamental peppers (*Capsicum annuum*), sansevierias and tradescantias, could be positioned on or close to an east- or west-facing windowsill, where they will probably not need protecting from the sun. Other types such as bomeliads, ivies and peperomias, which like a bright but sunless position, may be placed near to, but not in front of, a bright window or on a north-facing windowsill or one that is obscured from full sun, perhaps by a nearby wall or fence.

A position near to, but not in front of, a sunless window or one some way from a bright window, by which distance the light intensity will have dropped considerably, is suitable for a bottle garden containing ferns and other semi-shade loving plants such as fittonias and ivies. Plants in this category may also be grown in conditions classed as "shade", in a position well away from a window, although it may be advisable to move them closer to the light in winter. The test is that if there is enough light for you to read a newspaper, shade-loving plants should be happy.

These broad outlines of light and shady conditions presuppose that the container, in the case of a terrarium, is made of clear glass, which allows maximum light penetration. If a green glass bottle is planted, you can estimate that the coloured material will filter out about half of the available light. If you were to position the bottle garden in a dimly lit situation the plants would have a considerable struggle to live up to your expectations. Even so, a terrarium should not be placed in direct, strong sunlight, because although this may be suitable in terms of light, it could cause an excessive build-up of heat inside the glass and scorch the plants.

If you want to grow plants that are attracted to bright light and cannot provide the requisite amount of daylight, you may want to consider the installation of some form of artificial lighting. The only difference the plants may notice between natural and artificial light is that the latter does not automatically allow them a period of rest in the winter, but that can be arranged with a flick of a switch.

Among the easiest lights to install are bulbs purpose-made to fit into most standard bayonet and screw light fittings and which, although costing more, use no more electricity than a normal bulb. These bulbs provide a cool, diffuse, colour-balanced light, which is suitable for healthy plant growth. There are two types of lamp – one designed for green foliage house

WINTER LIGHTING

I n winter you may want to consider moving a terrarium or dish garden nearer to a window. Remember that different kinds of plants have different requirements – variegated leaves, for example, need more light than, say, bromeliads – and you must bear these various requirements in mind when you position the containers. Remember, too, that green or tinted glass containers should be nearer to a light source than those made of clear glass.

direct winter sunshine

LEFT A coloured glass container can withstand a direct source of light.

RIGHT The glint of polished glass under a spotlight is a flattering setting for a plant collection. Do not choose a dark background, however, if the situation is poorly lit.

plants, which will generally tolerate poorer conditions, and the other for those more demanding tropical, coloured, richly variegated and flowering subjects. Both may be bought at garden centres, DIY stores and electrical shops.

If your dish garden contains a collection of orchids, bromeliads, peperomias or African violets you can encourage them to flower almost all the year round by installing more elaborate electrical equipment that will transform a shady room, which would normally be inhospitable to them, into an ideal environment. You could mount one or more fluorescent tubes under a reflector and fix them permanently above the growing surface. Calculate that you need to provide about 20 Watts per sq ft/0.09 sq m of growing area. If the unit is suspended on a device that can be raised or lowered, bringing the light and heat of the tubes closer to, or further away from, the plants, it can be all the more versatile. Watch the plants in the dish garden carefully to check that the artificial conditions are suitable. Signs of scorching on the leaves will indicate that the light source is too close to the plants. Pick off the damaged leaves and slightly raise the lighting unit. Plants that become spindly or whose leaves lose colour are a sure sign of insufficient light, so lower the unit a little.

Some everyday household factors can affect the quality of life of your indoor plants, too – even the colour of your walls and, dare it be said, the dust on your windows. If the light meter test shows that there is insufficient light in one room, you might find a more suitable situation for a dish garden or terrarium in a room with walls of a lighter colour. White, pale cream and off-white walls and ceilings, which reflect all the available light, can improve the health of the plants by a considerable amount. In addition, a pale background will reduce the tendency of plants' stems to bend towards the light source, which could be an important consideration if you have planted a terrarium or dish garden to have a "best" viewing side. Dusty windows can act like a filter and cut down the intensity of the light reaching the plants by as much as 10 per cent, which could be critical.

TEMPERATURE AND HUMIDITY

Plants in the sealed environment of a terrarium or a bottle garden are largely insulated from the rapid temperature changes that can cause severe problems with unprotected house plants, and they are also protected from draughts, another health hazard. At night, especially in the winter, when the room temperatures are likely to drop rapidly, sealed containers protect the plants, since the air in

BELOW Plants in sealed containers are less vulnerable to external changes in temperature or humidity. A sealed garden would, therefore, do well in a bathroom.

the bottles takes longer to cool than that on the outside.

Plants in sealed containers have an advantage in humidity terms, too, and are unaffected by the dryness in the atmosphere that is caused by central heating. If your plants are grown in a dish garden or as a collection in an open container they will create their own micro-climate, which is more favourable than that created by a single pot plant. Even so, unless you have a room humidifier installed for your own comfort, you may need to increase the localized humidity for some plants. Spraying the leaves with a fine mist spray of cool, but not ice-cold, water is usually enough, although this treatment is not recommended for furry-leaved plants such as African violets and those with paper-thin leaves such as maidenhair ferns.

Enclosed plants are more likely to suffer from the heat and intensity of the summer sun than the cold in the winter. Few of us are prepared or able to tolerate room temperatures so low that they would spell disaster to terrarium plants and so, with our own well-being in mind, we are unlikely to present them with an uncompromisingly hostile environment. Such conditions can arise in winter, however, when a terrarium is positioned on a windowsill on the "wrong" side of the curtains at night so that it is insulated from the comparative warmth of the room. If it is not possible to move the terrarium into the room – and its weight and size may prevent this – you should improvise some form of insulation against the window. You may be able to rest a piece of polystyrene or a wooden board against the glass at night and so raise the temperature by a vital few degrees.

Perhaps surprisingly, since they are often thought of as exotic plants, cacti and succulents can withstand extremes of temperature, although not draughts. In their natural habitat,

RIGHT Viewed from above, as it is when placed on a low table, this shallow glass fruit bowl makes a colourful display. (From the side the planting medium steals the scene.) There are two varieties of polka-dot plants *(Hypoestes sanguinolenta)*, a Kentia palm *(Howea forsteriana)*, a brake fern *(Pteris cretica* var. *cristata)*, a variegated ivy *(Hedera helix)*, and a miniature creeping fig *(Ficus pumila* "Minima"*)*.

the desert, they are adapted to survive the contrast of hot days and cold nights, and they have no problem with the see-sawing temperatures experienced in some centrally heated homes.

THE PERFECT BACKGROUND

Lighting and heating are not the only considerations that are likely to contribute to the healthy development of the plants. You must also look at indoor gardens in terms of their decorative properties, which is, of course, why many people decide to cultivate them. The sight of a pale green glass bottle garden on a low table, hazy with yellow shafts of winter sunshine, is a therapeutic one indeed, the more so when the inclemency of the weather makes gardening out of doors a chilling prospect.

We have already noted that positioning a terrarium or dish garden against a pale-coloured wall can help to increase the amount

RIGHT The tinted glass panels of this leaded terrarium look most attractive when the light from an artificial source or the sun shines through them. The polka-dot plant, with its reddish-pink leaves, has been selected to complement the colour of the glass.

of light that reaches the plants, but the matter of background colour does not end there. If you are to see your indoor garden to the best decorative advantage, it is important to take account of the colours, patterns and textures that surround it. Think of the wall, table or curtain material as a frame for the indoor garden and do your best to make it as flattering a background as possible.

Usually a terrarium or bottle garden made of green-tinted glass and almost certainly planted with several green foliage plants will look best against a plain and contrasting background. Stand a terrarium on a large, square coffee table, for example, where it will be viewed mainly from above but also from all sides, and the wood will largely frame the container and also add to the natural appearance of the group. If the carpet happens to be heavily patterned, the area of the table should intervene and isolate the plants from the potential distraction of the floor covering. If, on the other hand, the terrarium stands on a small, low pedestal table against a similarly colourful background, the beauty and tranquillity of the plants might well be overwhelmed by the competition.

The same may be said of a strongly patterned wallcovering or curtain material, especially one that is composed predominantly of flowers or foliage. The clearly defined outline of a green glass bottle garden may be strong enough to stand out against the pattern, but the plants inside would almost certainly be difficult to distinguish. A dish garden, which does not have the benefit of the container surrounding it, might have even more of a visual battle. Try to imagine a long, low trough luxuriously planted with coral, pink and white orchids such as *Phalaenopsis* and *Miltonia* displayed against a wallpaper covered in red and pink rambler roses.

Whenever possible, then, you should try to place an indoor garden against a plain background or one that has a subtle or restrained pattern. A contrast in both colour and tone is also advisable. However aesthetically pleasing a green-on-green composition may be, if you place a green bottle garden against a mid-green wall, the foliage plants may be virtually indistinguishable. If, however, the terrarium is planted with red and carmine foliage plants, green may well be the best background colour choice, since red and

BELOW A low coffee table or dressing-table is ideal for this squat, square jar planted with a Victorian favourite, creeping moss, a member of the *Selaginella* genus.

its size. That would be visually most unappealing so avoid it if you can.

Using mirror glass in this way enables you to enjoy a terrarium or dish garden from both the front and the rear aspect at the same time – a point that should be taken into consideration when planting. It also increases the intensity of light that reaches the plant, since reflected light is just as effective as a primary light source in promoting plant health and growth.

A horizontal mirror surface can be an effective stand for an indoor garden, especially for one that includes a number of trailing plants. If you have a coffee table or a dressing-table with a mirror-glass top, this could be an ideal place for a shallow bowl of trailing ivies or a brandy snifter spilling over with a miniature creeping fig (Ficus pumila "Minima").

Putting your plants on a pedestal is another way to enjoy a comprehensive under-view of an indoor garden. A round or hexagonal leaded terrarium, a bottle garden or a Victorian-style bell-jar arrangement are all suitable for an elevated position of this kind. The viewing angle enables you to appreciate the beauty of small and delicate ground-cover plants such as mosses and fittonias, and the height above the ground may mean that the indoor garden is attractively back-lit by light from a window or lamp. You could use a simple wooden or wrought-iron pedestal of the kind that are available from some florists' shops or a simulated stone one from a garden supply shop. Do make sure that the top of the pedestal is large enough to support the indoor garden securely. If it is not, you could attach a larger board so that the terrarium was surrounded on all sides. And do make sure that any pedestal is safely out of the way of through traffic, particularly if there are children, elderly people or boisterous pets in your home.

ABOVE A tasteful home-made terrarium containing a young philodendron and dwarf *sansevieria*.

green are complementary colours, each emphasizing the shades, tints and tones of the other.

You could double the visual pleasure you derive from one indoor garden by placing it against a large wall mirror. You may be able to find an old wooden or even a gilded frame and have a piece of looking glass cut to fit, or you could buy an inexpensive mirror in a simple softwood frame. Make sure that the glass is in proportion to the indoor garden and has space to spare on all sides. It would look like the compromise that it is to have a conservatory-shaped terrarium placed against a mirror half

CHAPTER SIX

Planning and Planting ~Do's and Don'ts

An at-a-glance list of points to remember when planning, planting and maintaining your terrarium or dish garden.

DO select plants that are appropriate to the conditions you can offer them.

DO check the specific requirements of each plant before you buy it. The Directory at the end of the book includes the information you will need.

DO buy small plants, known in the trade as "tots". Not only will you have the pleasure of watching them develop, but it will be a long time before they outgrow the container and you will need to replace them.

DO select plants that have similar requirements in terms of light, heat and moisture so that they can exist healthily together.

DO make sure that the plants you buy are free from pests. The introduction of a single plant carrying, for example, whitefly will affect your whole collection.

DO use a sterilized peat- or loam-based compost. Unsterilized soil is a sure way of introducing pests and diseases.

DO be adventurous when planting a terrarium or fish tank garden. Such a favourable micro-climate is wasted on everyday plants. Consider growing orchids, cryptanthus, calatheas, crotons, bromeliads and others you will find described in the Directory.

DO try to introduce some colours other than green into your terrarium or bottle garden. African violets, small orchids and red-leaved plants add enormously to the appeal.

DO NOT overcrowd the terrarium or bottle garden with too many plants. Using rocks, stones, shells and other accessories to separate plants helps to avoid this temptation and adds to the natural appearance of the group.

DO NOT skimp on the drainage layers or your indoor garden will become waterlogged. Any terrarium or dish garden that does not have drainage holes will need a base layer of gravel or grit and one of broken charcoal.

DO NOT position plants so that they will be crushed against the glass of a terrarium or they may soon become diseased.

DO consider using artificial lighting in one form or another.

DO learn to recognize the "danger signals" that indicate inappropriate lighting levels.

DO remember that the duration as well as the intensity of the light affects plant growth. In the growing season most plants need 12–16 hours of natural light or the equivalent artificial light.

DO remember that flowering plants will suffer most if they are deprived of adequate lighting; in fact, they may cease to be flowering plants at all.

DO give indoor gardens composed of cacti and other succulents priority in lighting terms. They have the highest light requirement of all.

DO NOT install electrical fittings unless you are competent to do so. If you are not, ask an electrician.

DO NOT place a terrarium in direct mid-summer sunshine. The plants will become overheated and scorched.

DO NOT expose your plants to more light than they need because this can result in scorched patches on leaves, leaves that wilt at midday, when the sun is strongest, leaves that have a "washed-out" look and leaves that will shrivel and die.

DO NOT expect your plants to thrive with too little light. This may result in variegated leaves, which need the most light, losing their dual

LEFT Polish lack-lustre leaves with a proprietary leafshine liquid, applied with a soft cloth or tissue.

colouring, in lower leaves and flowers being smaller than normal and in spindly growth between the leaves.

DO NOT subject your indoor garden to a culture shock by suddenly moving it from one extreme of light to another, from a shady corner to a sunny windowsill. Move it into partial shade for a few days so that the plants can become acclimatized.

FRESH AIR AND HUMIDITY

DO give plants that are not in sealed containers an occasional breath of fresh air by taking them outdoors in summer or by opening a window. Cacti and succulents in particular respond well to the treatment, and forest cacti actually need to be stood outdoors during the summer months.

DO mist-spray plants in open containers to keep up the humidity level. Plants with papery leaves need more humidity in the air than ones with thick, leathery leaves.

DO be prepared to move an open garden dish from one room to another if problems arise. For example, if a centrally heated living-room has minimal humidity, a spell in an occasionally steamy bathroom could work wonders.

DO consider the bathroom as a friendly habitat for your indoor gardens. A large terrarium looks completely at home on the floor or on a low table, while a small one would suit a windowsill. If the room is warm and in frequent use it could be the ideal habitat for ferns and ivies.

DO NOT overdo the humidity. Too much moisture can cause patches of grey mould or rot on the leaves – the stem ends are usually attacked first – and on flowers. Cacti and succulents are particularly susceptible to excessive humidity.

DO NOT include cacti and succulents in a terrarium or aquarium garden. They cannot tolerate the humidity.

DO give plants that need it a complete rest in winter, when their growth slows down and may stop. Plants grown in open containers may need watering only one to three times a month throughout winter.

ABOVE Plants in an open container will need more frequent watering than those in a sealed one. Even so, water them sparingly.

DO use rainwater if your tap water is especially hard. Hard water sometimes causes a white crust to form on the surface of the compost, which, although not harmful, can be unsightly.

DO remember that the roots of all plants, except aquatic ones, need air as well as water. That is why the compost should be kept only moist, not saturated.

DO learn to recognize the effects of over-watering plants before it is too late. The flowers may go mouldy, and the leaves become soft, limp, yellow or wilted. Leaf tips may turn brown, and both young and mature leaves fall at the same time.

DO take care not to let the reverse happen. Signs of too little water are that the oldest leaves fall first, flowers quickly fade and fall, and leaves wilt and become limp.

DO learn to feed plants on demand. Once the supply of nutrients in the compost is exhausted, which may be two months after planting, some feeding may be needed throughout the growing season – that is, from spring to autumn for most flowering and foliage plants, and during winter only for winter-flowering ones.

DO get to know your plants' dietary requirements. Nitrogen is known as the leaf maker, phosphates promote healthy root growth, and potash feeds the flowers. Most proprietary house plant foods contain all three, and some also contain trace elements, which are derived from humus extracts or added chemicals.

DO NOT over-water plants in a terrarium or dish garden. That is the most usual cause of disappointment.

DO NOT water plants in the full glare of the sun. Splashes on the leaves may cause scorch marks.

DO NOT use ice-cold water to freshen your indoor garden. It is best to leave it to stand indoors overnight, and that also allows it to lose some of the chlorine.

DO NOT spoil your plants by over-feeding them. Too much fertilizer causes brown spots and shrivelled edges on leaves, stunted growth in summer and a white crust on the surface of the compost.

ABOVE Cut off any leaves that would come into contact with the glass; they would eventually become damaged.

DO take a pride in the appearance of your plants and pick or cut off any damaged or discoloured leaves and the flowers as soon as they start to fade. Especially in a terrarium, fallen leaves and flowers may rot and cause other plants to become infected.

DO keep the surface of leaves clean and free from dust, which clogs the leaf pores and blocks out the light. Syringe or sponge the leaves – although do not do this to furry ones – with clean water early in the day so that they will dry before the temperature drops at night. Cacti, succulents and hairy leaves should not be sprayed or washed – dust them with a soft brush.

DO notice when leaves become lack-lustre and dull. You can restore their sheen by applying a proprietary leafshine liquid on a piece of cotton wool. Do not polish very young, hairy or furry leaves.

DO cut off any dead or diseased stems, leaves that are crowding the plant – an important consideration in a container of limited size – and any all-green shoots that appear on variegated plants.

DO pinch out the growing stems of vigorous plants such as tradescantia to encourage more bushy growth and branching. Use your fingers, scissors or a razor blade to "stop" stems that have at least three leaves. Do this only during the growing period.

DO cut back any stems that bear abnormally small or pale leaves. This can occur with ivies that have been kept too warm during the winter. This irregular growth will detract from the beauty of your terrarium or dish garden.

DO NOT polish leaves with olive oil, an old-fashioned method. It does produce a satisfactory sheen, but leaves a sticky deposit that attracts dust. And then you are back to square one.

SITING

DO welcome your guests with a terrarium or dish garden in a covered porch or in the hall if the lighting is adequate. An early example of your gardening talents will become an immediate talking point.

DO consider planting terrariums or bottle gardens in pairs. This two-by-two approach to display is especially effective on either side of an arch, a doorway, a statue or an aquarium.

DO treat yourself to a terrarium or dish garden in the bedroom. A bottle garden displayed on a blanket box in front of a window or at the foot of a bed, a small Victoria dome garden on a bedside table, a dish garden of flowering cacti on the windowsill – many people find growing plants in the bedroom soothing and relaxing.

DO consider suspending plant groups from the ceiling if there is no space on the floor or a table-top. A small green glass bottle garden looks elegant if unusual when it is held in a macramé basket hanging from a hook, especially if it is suspended in front of a window.

DO NOT forget the dining-table as a showplace for a terrarium, a group of plants or a dish garden. They are all types of flower arrangements at the ready, and can make delightful centrepieces.

CHAPTER SEVEN

Plant Directory

se this directory as a guide to some of the many plants you can grow in a terrarium, in an open container or a dish garden. There are many, many more plants that will thrive in enclosed containers and dish gardens than can be listed here, so do experiment.

The heights given are approximate. They will depend on the conditions under which the plants are grown, and on how much you allow them to develop or how much you prune them to restrict growth.

The references to the minimum temperature requirements are: warm – 13–16°C (55–61°F);

moderate – 7.5–13°C (45–55°F); and cool – 4.5–7.5°C (40–45°F).

The references to humidity requirements are: high – above 70 per cent on a hygrometer, the conditions provided by a terrarium; medium – 40–70 per cent, achieved by growing several plants with some additional source of humidity such as a moist gravel tray; and low – below 40 per cent, conditions that might prevail in an ordinary heated room.

When you buy plants for terrariums look out for dwarf varieties, which often have "Nana" in their names and for varieties with variegated and bi- and tri-coloured foliage.

PLANT	TYPE	FLOWER	HEIGHT	HUMIDITY	WATER	LIGHT	TEMP
Achimenes (Cupid's bower, hot-water plant)	Flowering, hairy leaves	Red, pink, purple, yellow, white, some bi-colours	30cm/12in	Medium; do not mist leaves	Keep compost moist from spring until end of flowering season	Bright	Warm
Acorus gramineus "Variegatus"	Grass, variegated	—	38cm/15in	Medium; thrives in terrarium	Keep moist	Bright or partial shade	Cool, unheated room in winter
Adiantum hispidulum (Australian maidenhair fern)	Fern	—	38cm/15in	High; ideal for terrarium	Keep moist	Bright or partial shade	Warm
Adiantum raddianum (delta maidenhair fern)	Fern	—	30cm/12in	High; ideal for terrarium	Keep moist	Bright or partial shade	Warm
Aechmea "Foster's Favorite" (lacquered wine-cup)	Flowering bromeliad with red foliage	Coral pink	30cm/12in	Medium; mist leaves in summer	Do not over-water; use soft water	Bright	High or warm
Agave victoriae-reginae (royal agave)	Succulent	—	15cm/6in	Low; do not mist leaves	Medium; in winter, only once every 1–2 months	Bright	Warm in summer; cool in winter
Ajuga reptans "Variegata" (bugle)	Ground-cover; red-purple foliage	Blue spikes	7.5cm/3in	Low	Medium	Bright	Warm

PLANT	TYPE	FLOWER	HEIGHT	HUMIDITY	WATER	LIGHT	TEMP
Allium schoenoprasum (chives)	Flowering herb with grass-like leaves	Pink, mauve	23cm/9in	Medium	Keep moist	Bright or partial shade	Warm
Aloe variegata (partridge-breasted aloe)	Succulent	—	15cm/6in	Low; do not mist leaves	Medium; in winter, only once every 1–2 months	Bright	Warm in summer, cool in winter
Anthemis nobilis (camomile)	Flowering herb, with feathery leaves	Cream, white	30cm/12in	Low	Medium	Sunny and bright	Warm
Arabis caucasica A. albida	Flowering alpine	White	12cm/5in	Low	Keep moist	Sunny	Warm
Araucaria heterophylla (Norfolk Island pine)	Conifer	—	Use seedlings in terrarium	Medium	Keep moist	Bright or partial shade	Warm in summer, cool in winter
Asparagus densiflorus/ A. sprengeri (emerald fern)	Fern-like	—	30cm/12in	Medium; mist occasionally	Regularly in summer, sparingly in winter	Bright or partial shade	Moderate
Asplenium bulbiferum (mother spleenwort, hen-and-chicken fern)	Fern	—	38cm/15in	High	Keep moist	Partial shade	Moderate
Astilbe chinensis "Pumila"	Flowering alpine	Pink	30cm/12in	High; mist leaves occasionally	Keep moist	Bright or partial shade	Cool
Aubrieta	Ground-cover, flowering	White, pink, purple, blue	7.5cm/3in	Low	Medium	Sunny	Warm
Beloperone guttata/ Justicia brandegeana (shrimp plant)	Flowering; downy leaves	Salmon pink	15cm/6in	Medium; mist leaves occasionally	Keep moist until winter, then sparingly	Sunny, bright	Warm in summer, cool in winter
Calendula officinalis (pot marigold)	Flowering hardy annual	Yellow or orange	23cm/9in	Medium	Medium	Sunny, bright or partial shade	Warm

A thick cluster of chives topped by their pinky-mauve flowers adds colour and volume to a dish garden.

PLANT	TYPE	FLOWER	HEIGHT	HUMIDITY	WATER	LIGHT	TEMP
Campanula isophylla (Italian bellflower)	Flowering	White, blue, mauve	15cm/6in	Medium; mist leaves occasionally	Keep moist during summer	Bright	Warm or cool
Capsicum annuum (ornamental pepper)	Flowering and fruiting	Red and yellow fruits	23cm/9in	Medium to high; mist leaves often	Keep moist	Bright	Warm or cool
Carex morrowii/ C. oshnimensis "Variegata" (Japanese sedge)	Grass	—	38cm/15in	Medium	Permanently moist, but not wet	Bright or partial shade	Cool
Catharanthus roseus/ Vinca rosea (rose periwinkle)	Flowering annual	White, pink, mauve	20cm/8in	Medium	Keep permanently moist	Bright	Moderate
Chamaecyparis obtusa "Nana gracilis" (Hinoki cypress)	Conifer	—	2m/6ft	Low	Keep moist	Sunny or partial shade	Warm
Chamaedorea elegans/ Neanthe bella (parlour palm, dwarf mountain palm)	Palm	—	38cm/15in	High; mist if leaves grow in open	Keep only slightly moist	Partial shade	Warm
Chlorophytum comosum (spider plant)	Foliage, variegated, trailing	—	30cm/12in	Medium; mist leaves in summer	Keep moist in summer	Bright	Cool
Chrysanthemum parthenium (feverfew)	Flowering perennial	White, cream	23cm/9in	Medium	Medium but never wet	Sunny, bright	Warm
Codiaeum variegatum (croton)	Flowering, variegated	—	38cm/15in	High; mist leaves frequently	Keep moist until winter, then sparingly	Bright	Warm
Columnea crassifolia	Flowering	Red, tubular	30cm/12in	Medium; mist leaves often	Keep moist in summer	Bright	Warm
Cordyline terminalis/ C. fruticosa "Red Page" (goodluck plant, ti tree)	False palm	—	30cm/12in	High; mist leaves often	Keep slightly moist	Partial shade	Warm

The *Neanthe bella* produces small yellow flowers, but its chief attraction is its mass of green leaves.

PLANT	TYPE	FLOWER	HEIGHT	HUMIDITY	WATER	LIGHT	TEMP
Crassula arborescens (silver jade plant)	Succulent, grey, green leaves	Varied	38cm/15in	Low; needs fresh air	Water only when compost dries out; infrequently in winter	Sunny	Warm in summer, cool in winter
Crossandra undulifolia/ C. infundibuliformis (firecracker flower)	Flowering	Orange, red	38cm/15in	High; mist leaves often	Keep moist in summer	Bright	Warm
Cryptanthus (earth star)	Bromeliad, dramatic foliage	Various	From 10cm/4in	High; ideal for terrariums	Keep moist, use soft water	Bright	High
Cycas revoluta (Japanese sago palm)	False palm	—	3m/10ft	High	Keep only slightly moist	Partial shade	Warm; avoid draughts
Cymbidium (Boat orchid)	Flowering orchid	Various	Some miniature, 15cm/6in	High; mist leaves occasionally	Keep moist	Partial shade	High or warm; cool at night
Cyperus alternifolius (umbella plant)	Foliage, grass-like	—	43cm/17in	High; mist leaves often if grown in open	Keep moist	Partial shade	Warm or cool
Cyrtomium falcatum "Rock fordianum" (holly fern, fishtail fern)	Fern	—	30–60cm/ 12–24in	High; ideal for terrarium	Keep moist	Bright or partial shade	Warm
Davallia canariensis (hare's foot fern)	Fern	—	30cm/12in	High	Keep moist	Bright or partial shade	Warm
Dianthus caryophyllus (clove pink)	Flowering perennial, silver leaves	Scented, pink and other colours, many bi-coloured	30cm/12in	Medium or low	Medium	Sunny and bright	Warm
Dracaena	Foliage, many are variegated	—	60cm/24in	High; mist leaves often if grown in open	Keep moist, even in winter	Light shade	Warm
Echinofossulocactus zacatecasensis (brain cactus)	Cactus	—	15cm/6in globe	Low; likes fresh air	Medium	Sunny	Warm

The bromeliad group of plants includes many with dramatically striped leaves. These two varieties of earth star (*Cryptanthus*) are best suited to planting in enclosed containers.

The red-striped Madagascar dragon tree (*Dracaena marginata*) is planted in the green bottle garden shown in chapter two.

PLANT	TYPE	FLOWER	HEIGHT	HUMIDITY	WATER	LIGHT	TEMP
Epiphyllum ackermannii/ Nopalxochia ackermannii (red orchid cactus)	Cactus, forest-type, flowering	Bright red	30cm/12in	Medium	Medium; none in winter	Sunny and bright	Warm
Episcia cupreata (flame violet)	Flowering, with wrinkled, variegated leaves	Bright red	15cm/6in	High; ideal for terrarium	Keep moist, even in winter	Sunny and bright	Warm
Erica gracilis (Cape heath)	Flowering, in autumn and winter	Red, pink, purple, small globular	25cm/10in	High; mist leaves often	Keep moist; use soft water or rain-water	Sunny and bright, or partial shade	Cool, especially in flowering season
Erinus alpinus	Flowering alpine	Pink	5cm/2in	Low	Medium	Sunny	Warm
Erodium chrysanthemum	Flowering alpine	Cream	23cm/9in	Low	Medium	Sunny	Warm
Euonymus japonicus "Microphyllus" (Japanese spindle)	Variegated foliage, flowering	Small white	30–90cm/1–3ft	Low	Medium	Bright or partial shade	Warm or cool
Exacum affine (Persian or Arabian violet)	Flowering	Pink, mauve	30cm/12in	High; mist leaves often	Keep moist at all times	Bright	Warm or cool
Ficus pumila "Minima" (creeping fig)	Foliage	—	10cm/4in	High	Allow compost to dry	Bright	Warm
Fittonia verschaffeltii var. *argyroneura* "Nana" (silver net leaf)	Foliage, creeper	—	10cm/4in	High; ideal for terrarium	Keep moist in summer, sparingly in winter	Partial shade	Warm
Gymnocalycium mihanovichii var. *hibotan* (hibotan cactus)	Flowering cactus	Red	10cm/4in	Low; needs fresh air	Little	Sunny	Warm
Gynura sarmentosa (velvet plant, purple passion)	Flowering, variegated foliage	Small yellow, unpleasant smell	60cm/2ft or more	Medium; mist leaves occasionally	Keep moist in summer, sparingly in winter	Sunny and bright	Warm
Hebe pimelioides "Glauca" (hebe)	Flowering; blue-green foliage	Pink spikes	15cm/6in	Low	Keep moist	Sunny and bright	Warm

The bright scarlet dome of the hibotan cactus (*Gymnocalycium mihanovichii* var. *hibotan*) makes a brilliant focal point in any group.

PLANT	TYPE	FLOWER	HEIGHT	HUMIDITY	WATER	LIGHT	TEMP
Hedera helix (ivy)	Foliage, some variegated	—	15cm/6in	High; mist leaves frequently	Keep moist in summer, sparingly in winter	Bright	Cool
Helxine soleirolii/ Soleirolia soleirolii (mind-your-own-business, baby's tears)	Foliage, yellow, green or silver-grey	—	7.5cm/3in	High; mist leaves often	Keep moist in summer, sparingly in winter	Bright or partial shade	Warm
Howea forsteriana (kentia palm)	Palm	—	10m/30ft	High; mist leaves if not in a terrarium	Good drainage essential; keep only slightly moist in winter	Partial shade	Medium; avoid draughts
Hypocyrta nummularia/ Alloplectus nummularia (clog plant)	Flowering	Orange	7.5cm/3in	Medium	Medium	Bright or partial shade	Warm
Hypoestes sanguinolenta/ H. phyllostachya (polka-dot plant)	Foliage, spotted	—	20cm/8in	Medium; mist leaves often	Keep moist	Bright or partial shade	Warm
Impatiens (busy lizzie)	Flowering, some with variegated foliage	Pink, red, orange, white, some bi-colour	20cm/8in	Medium; can mist leaves but not flowers	Keep moist	Bright or partial shade	Warm
Iresine herbstii (blood leaf, beefsteak plant)	Foliage, bright red	—	30cm/12in	High	Medium	Bright	Warm
Kalanchoë blossfeldiana (flaming Katy)	Succulent, flowering all year	Red, pink	30cm/12in	Low; do not mist	Allow compost to dry	Bright or partial shade	Warm
Laurus nobilis (bay laurel, sweet bay)	Shrub, fragrant leaves	Minute white	Keep well pruned to modify	Medium; mist leaves often	Medium	Sunny	Cool or warm
Lavandula (lavender)	Flowering herb	Mauve, blue, purple	30cm/12in	Low	Low–medium	Sunny	Warm
Leucanthemum hosmariense/ Chrysanthemum hosmariense	Flowering shrublet	White, daisy-like	15cm/6in	Low	Medium	Sunny	Warm

Hypoestes sanguinolenta, which has popular names such as polka-dot plant and freckle face, is frequently included in terrarium groups for the splash of colour variation it brings.

There are several varieties of *Kalanchoë blossfeldiana*, colourful succulents that may have yellow, pink, crimson or scarlet flowers.

With its hoop of minute pink flowers, *Mammillaria bocasana* adds a brilliant colour highlight.

The Tom Thumb cactus (*Parodia sanguiniflora*), with its bright red, papery flowers, brings an exotic splash of colour to any group.

PLANT	TYPE	FLOWER	HEIGHT	HUMIDITY	WATER	LIGHT	TEMP
Lithops lesliei (living stones)	Stone-like succulent	Yellow	5cm/2in	Low	Little	Sunny or bright	Warm
Lobivia aurea/ Echinopsis aurea (golden lily cactus)	Cactus	Yellow	15cm/6in	Low	Medium	Sunny	Warm
Mammillaria bocasana (powder-puff cactus)	Cactus	White, pink	15cm/6in globe	Low	Medium	Sunny	Warm
Maranta leuconeura (prayer plant)	Foliage, variegated and multi-coloured	—	20cm/8in	High; mist leaves often	Keep moist	Partial shade	Warm; avoid draughts
Mimosa pudica (sensitive plant, humble plant)	Foliage folds up when touched	—	30cm/12in	High	Medium	Bright	Warm
Mimulus primuloides (musk)	Flowering alpine	Yellow	7.5cm/3in	Low	Keep moist	Sunny	Warm
Nephrolepis spp.	Fern	—	30cm/12in	High	Keep moist	Partial shade	Warm
Ocimum basilicum (basil)	Annual herb	Insignificant	30cm/12in	Low	Keep moist in summer	Sunny	Warm
Odontoglossum (tiger orchid)	Flowering	Various	38cm/15in	High	Keep moist	Partial shade	High or warm, cool at night
Opuntia microdasys (bunny ears)	Cactus	—	30cm/12in	Low	Medium	Sunny	Warm
Origanum marjorana (sweet marjoram)	Herb, flowering	Mauve, pink	30cm/12in	Low	Medium	Sunny	Warm
Paphiopedilum (slipper orchid)	Flowering	Various, spotted and striped	38cm/15in	High; mist leaves occasionally	Keep moist	Partial shade	High or warm; cool at night
Parodia sanguiniflora	Cactus	Red, daisy-like	12.5cm/5in	Low; open windows in summer	Use tepid water; keep almost dry in winter	Sunny	Medium-cool in winter
Pellaea rotundifolia (button fern)	Fern	—	15cm/6in	Medium	Low (unusually for ferns)	Partial shade	Warm

PLANT	TYPE	FLOWER	HEIGHT	HUMIDITY	WATER	LIGHT	TEMP
Pellionia daveauana/ *P. repens* (watermelon begonia)	Foliage	—	10cm/4in	High	Medium	Bright or partial shade	Warm
Peperomia spp.	Flowering, some variegated foliage	Green	15cm/6in	Medium; mist leaves in summer only	Allow compost to dry; use tepid water	Bright or partial shade	Warm
Petroselinum crispum (parsley)	Herb	Insignificant	30cm/12in	Low; take outdoors often in summer	Keep moist	Sunny	Warm
Phalaenopsis (moth orchid)	Flowering	Various, spotted	38cm/15in	High; mist leaves occasionally	Keep moist	Partial shade	High or warm; cool at night
Pilea cadierei (aluminium plant)	Foliage, variegated	Insignificant	30cm/12in	High; mist leaves often	Allow compost to dry, then water liberally	Bright or partial shade	Warm
Piper ornatum (ornamental pepper)	Foliage	Red and green fruits	20cm/8in	High	Medium	Bright	Warm
Polystichum tsus-simense (holly fern)	Fern	—	23cm/9in	Medium or low	Medium	Partial shade	Warm
Pteris spp. (brake fern)	Fern	—	30cm/12in	High	Keep moist	Partial shade	Warm
Rebutia minuscula (Mexican sunball)	Cactus	Red	5cm/2in	Low	Medium	Sunny	Warm
Rhoeo discolor/ *Tradescantia spathacea* (boat lily, Moses-in-the-cradle)	Flowering	Whitish	50cm/20in	High	Medium	Bright or partial shade	Warm
Saintpaulia ionantha (African violet)	Flowering for up to 10 months in year	Red, pink, white, some bi- and multi-coloured	15cm/6in	High; but do not mist	Allow compost surface to dry; use tepid water; needs feeding	Bright	Warm; avoid draughts
Sansevieria trifasciata (mother-in-law's tongue)	Foliage	—	60cm/24in	Medium	Medium; water around plant	Bright	Warm

African violets *(Saintpaulia)* are among the most popular house plants. They require a brightly lit situation and high humidity, and should be watered with tepid water. Do not allow water to get on the leaves.

PLANT	TYPE	FLOWER	HEIGHT	HUMIDITY	WATER	LIGHT	TEMP
Saxifraga (any variety)	Foliage	Mostly insignificant	7.5cm/3in	High; mist leaves occasionally	Keep moist in summer	Bright	Cool
Sedum (stonecrop)	Flowering alpine	White, yellow, blue, purple	10cm/4in	Low	Medium	Sunny	Warm
Selaginella kraussiana (creeping moss)	Foliage	—	7.5cm/3in	High; ideal for terrarium	Keep moist; use soft water	Semi-shade	Warm; avoid draughts
Siderasis fuscata (brown spiderwort)	Foliage	—	20cm/8in	High	Medium	Bright	Warm
Silene (any variety)	Flowering alpine	Pink, red, white	15cm/6in	Low	Medium	Sunny	Warm
Streptocarpus rexii (Cape primrose)	Flowering	Pink, mauve	20cm/8in	Medium	Medium	Bright	Warm
Syngonium podophyllum/ Nephthytis triphylla (goosefoot plant)	Foliage, climber	—	2m/6ft	High	Medium	Bright or partial shade	Warm
Tillandsia argentea (air plants)	Foliage; known as 'Grey Tillandsias'	Some flowering species	Various	High	None; they are not planted, but attached to wood, etc.	Partial shade	Warm
Tillandsia lindenii (blue-flowered torch)	Bromeliad, flowering	Blue	40cm/16in	Medium	Medium; use soft water	Bright	High or warm
Tolmiea menziesii (piggyback plant)	Foliage	—	45cm/18in	Medium; mist leaves occasionally	Keep moist	Shade or partial shade	Cool
Tradescantia group	Foliage	—	15cm/6in	Medium	Liberally spring to autumn; minimal in winter	Bright	Medium
Vriesea splendens (flaming sword)	Bromeliad, flowering	Red or yellow, sword-like	30cm/12in	Medium; mist leaves in summer	Medium	Bright	High or warm

The variegated leaves of different varieties of tradescantia look even more spectacular when they are viewed through glass.

Index

Page numbers in *italics* refer to illustration captions. **Bold** numbers refer to the Plant Directory.

INDEX